PLOUGH P9-AGM-270

Spring 2002 · Vol. 28, No. 1

GUEST EDITOR
Cornelius Eady

EDITOR
Don Lee

MANAGING EDITOR
Gregg Rosenblum

POETRY EDITOR
David Daniel

ASSOCIATE FICTION EDITOR
Maryanne O'Hara

ASSOCIATE POETRY EDITOR
Susan Conley

FOUNDING EDITOR
DeWitt Henry

FOUNDING PUBLISHER
Peter O'Malley

PLOUGHSHARES, a journal of new writing, is guest-edited serially by prominent writers who explore different and personal visions, aesthetics, and literary circles. PLOUGHSHARES is published in April, August, and December at Emerson College, 120 Boylston Street, Boston, MA 02116-4624. Telephone: (617) 824-8753. Web address: www.pshares.org.

ASSISTANT FICTION EDITORS: Jay Baron Nicorvo and Nicole Kelley. EDITORIAL ASSISTANTS: Megan Weireter and Aja DeKleva Cohen.

POETRY READERS: Simeon Berry, Erin Lavelle, Sean Singer, Joanne Diaz, and Jennifer Thurber. FICTION READERS: Simeon Berry, Erin Lavelle, Hannah Bottomy, Jeffrey Voccola, Wendy Wunder, Eson Kim, Coppelia Liebenthal, Michael Rainho, Cortney Hamilton, Lisa Dush, Laura Tarvin, Christopher Helmuth, and Susan Nusser.

SUBSCRIPTIONS (ISSN 0048-4474): $22 for one year (3 issues), $42 for two years (6 issues); $25 a year for institutions. Add $12 a year for international ($10 for Canada).

UPCOMING: Fall 2002, a fiction issue edited by Margot Livesey, will appear in August 2002. Winter 2002–03, a poetry and fiction issue edited by C. D. Wright, will appear in December 2002.

GUEST EDITOR POLICY: Please see page 212 for information.

SUBMISSIONS: Reading period is from August 1 to March 31 (postmark dates). All submissions sent from April to July are returned unread. Please see page 212 for detailed submission policies.

Back-issue, classroom-adoption, and bulk orders may be placed directly through PLOUGHSHARES. Microfilms of back issues may be obtained from University Microfilms. PLOUGHSHARES is also available as CD-ROM and full-text products from EBSCO, H.W. Wilson, Information Access, and UMI. Indexed in M.L.A. Bibliography, American Humanities Index, Index of American Periodical Verse, Book Review Index. Self-index through Volume 6 available from the publisher; annual supplements appear in the fourth number of each subsequent volume. The views and opinions expressed in this journal are solely those of the authors. All rights for individual works revert to the authors upon publication.

PLOUGHSHARES receives support from the Massachusetts Cultural Council and the National Endowment for the Arts.

Retail distribution by Bernhard DeBoer (Nutley, NJ) and Ingram Periodicals (La Vergne, TN). Printed in the U.S.A. on recycled paper by Capital City Press.

© 2002 by Emerson College   ISBN 0-933277-34-2

CONTENTS

Spring 2002

Cover art:
The Salamander by Jane Ehrlich
Oil on wood, 36″ x 50″, 1999

Ploughshares Patrons

This nonprofit publication would not be possible without the support of our readers and the generosity of the following individuals and organizations.

CORNELIUS EADY

Postcard from New York

February 2002

It's a different city now, this New York, the city my wife and I love (and choose) to live in, a new shorthand can be heard for time and location: "The Event," "The 11th," "The Pile." For weeks after, on the way to rehearsals for a play of mine that was going up, I would watch people slow down and gaze into the display window at the Job-Lot on the corner of 14th Street and University Place. There was a gas mask, at discount. I wondered what they were imagining—the shape of the toxic cloud, the half-second of calm before your nose tells you this scent isn't normal, everyday New York City funk? What were they supposing? And I wondered (and still think from time to time) what might have happened to the guy in the first tower those jets hit who called the local ABC station from his cell phone. He was up somewhere above the one-hundredth floor, above that horrible, smoking wound on the building. Everyone was fine, he wanted the rest of the city to know. Then, a few minutes later, the second plane hit the other tower, the one with all the broadcast antennas, and he was mute, and the rest of the city, without cable or police band radio, deaf and blind.

We rarely think of our lives as historical, yet suddenly, history was sifting down, on the leaves of the ginkgoes, on the roofs and hoods of our cars, into our startled noses, impossible to block out. It was all we could talk about. At the theater, on the bare stage, morning rehearsals would begin with a long talk about what this all meant, or was going to mean. It was hard to pretend, I thought, when you're surrounded by what you couldn't imagine. We all had theories; we didn't know. Like everyone else we were scared—and impatient—for what would come next. We were waiting for the new "normal" to show signs of appearing, if ever.

And within the context of the larger tragedy, Death kept up his other appointments; in my hometown of Rochester, New York, as the towers burned and fell, the second wife of one of the dearest people in my life was slowly turning into a widow, as she and her stepchildren and extended family drifted in the currents between the live television feed and her husband's deathbed. That weekend, as we drove north on the West Side Highway, on the way upstate to the memorial service, how normal the rest of the city looked—until we pulled upon the George Washington Bridge, and looked back, south, to that gray smudge that used to catch the light. And I wondered, Did my friend die, or escape?

A few weeks later, I'm on the roof of the poet Meg Kearney's apartment with another friend, Estha Brommer. We're on the Lower East Side, and, looking south, at night, there are two white pillars, klieg lights for the rescue workers and construction crews, burning into the sky where the towers once stood. This is *after*. Weeks of hoaxes, scares, alerts. Pox envelopes are winging their way through the postal system. We have seen the impossible: a fire that has burned for weeks (and will continue for months), a mayor, whose "tough love" attitude was about to assure that his exit from office would be as anonymous as possible, now forgiven, rehabilitated into being the right man at the right moment. It's a beautifully clear night in any other direction but south. As I look toward the site, I think, as I often have these days, of a snippet of a song by Paul Simon: *"Anger—and no one can heal it— slides through the metal detector."*

Meg, whose office-window view points straight to the site, something I used to envy a little, is reading aloud a new poem— one of the first I've heard on this topic that makes sense—called "View of Downtown Manhattan from My Bedroom," which she wrote the day after the 11th:

> The amputee insists
> her legs are still
> down there
>
> She feels them
> burning—
> She knows

When the smoke
clears they will be
standing

She's right, I think, and tell her; that's what it feels like. (*There it isn't,* my wife once said as we both looked down 7th Avenue one Sunday afternoon, fooled again by what we weren't seeing.) And then the three of us gazed out across the city, listening to the distant roar of traffic and airplanes, waiting for that other shoe to drop.

Since most of the writers in this issue submitted their work before last fall, you won't find anything here that addresses the World Trade Center, but you will find, I hope, in the stories and poems gathered, true human commerce, the witnessing of what has, and will hopefully continue, to go on between us. New York and America might be a different place, but if we're very lucky, this scary moment, with all its grief and contradictions, is being scribbled down right now by someone into our unofficial record.

Billy Strayhorn Writes "Lush Life"

Empty ice-cream carton
in a kitchen garbage can.
Up all night with your mother.
He beat her again. Up all night
eating ice cream, you made your mother laugh.

                    ly
Life   is lone

Duke's hands on your shoulders,
you play it again. Cancer
eats moth holes through
you and you and you.

                    ly
Life   is lone

Speeding upstate in the backseat,
on the Taconic, cocktail
in one hand, book in another
as autumn leaves blur by.
This life, New York, piano
love, then lonely, this life, love.

LINDA BAMBER

Familiarity

Teenagers for sure, one black, one white,
so when did they have that terrified, high-pigtailed
child? in yellow and pink,

screaming *Mommy, Mommy,*
at Sherman and Walden as I bike through.
The boy stands in the street, you'd say

irresolute, but his (good-looking) face is calm.
As if I were the child I see the mother's violent face
and then her back. *I won't take care of you,*

she shouts, and points to him and storms away.
Every bone in the child's body breaks from being dropped
or rather hurled, a clattering breakage of plates in flight.

I don't know you, man, says the boy from the street,
but doesn't leave, at least. I'm stupefied, straddling my bike
in glasses and mirror-rigged helmet, all this useless

apparatus on my head, devices for seeing
and not getting hurt. Everything that happens
all her life may have to pass through this

cool May 6 p.m., the dandelions in the sidewalk cracks,
the hardware store, the parking lot,
the biker like a staring bug.

Well, that's a woman's weapon, no?
Smash the thing you're known to care about;
rip the shirt you made yourself,

sob in front of guests.
It's over, asshole; YOU pick up the pieces.
Cry angrily while biking.

Will that show God (who made spring leaves)
how bitterly you disapprove
of his or her arrangements?

Academic in Traffic

Whether the language rebellion against phallogocentrism is really
the deepest thing
or whether it's just a way of getting out of history
i.e., race, class, and gender, so
tiresome, so unavoidable; whether, that is, poetry, etc.,
no matter how weird, surreal, anti-referential, disruptive, etc.,
accepts things as they are when they need to be changed? On

Mass. Ave. near the KFC,
"Some men see things as they are," a billboard thunder-snores,
"and say 'Why?' I see things as they might be and say,
'Why not?'" The tenants sued to get rid
of the billboards, the daily intrusion they made on their lives,
the lock on the door
picked or smashed and the false
authorities come as they please

leaving unflushed turds and mail on the floor,
opened, of course; the company countered by running
"public service" ads, like this one. It overlooks the square
like the optometrist's face in *Gatsby,* solemn, lying, supervisory.
Cars writhe and buck in its gaze. Elsewhere
a quote from Oliver Wendell Holmes, maybe smart
when he wrote it but
so stupid when displayed on high that

anarchists invaded it.
The group was called "Dare to Be Perky." (This is true.
I couldn't make it up.)
"When a man's mind has been stretched by a new idea," the ad
originally moaned, then blah and blahdy blah.
"When a man's anus has been stretched by a big penis…"
it perkily said when "Dare to Be Perky" was done—and my
brother, double-taking in traffic,

saw a mother covering
her children's eyes; —so we felt we were not alone
in thinking language matters. What are we doing, we who tend words?
Who read signs? Who read? Is it anything
to register these violations?
Is it anything to wait, in an agony of inactivity,
for language to arrive? What shall I tell my students?
Whatever I say they will part believe, part writhe under;
then they'll whirl off to their lives
like leaves; their historical lives.

Names

Along the Avenue of Sultans
   the beech and chestnuts
are dishabille from cold,
   ice-glazed, cloaked
in coal smoke from upended barrels
   the displaced huddle about.
The war is more elemental—
   stay warm, scrounge

for food, search photos posted
   everywhere for lost family:
Nedzad Ljuta, 55, last seen,
   Milo Medardich, 84, last seen,
Vinka Cickovic, 28, arrested,
   Alena Ramic, 14, brown hair,
green eyes, a schoolgirl, disappeared.
   Under the railway trestle

that crests the river, someone finds a boot
   with a severed foot inside.
Someone roasts a fish. An elderly man sobs,
   his breath a small ghost of mist.
One of the agencies will distribute more blankets,
   someone says, but it may be a rumor
to demoralize the people. A woman

builds a nest of torn cardboard and newspapers
   for two small children bundled
in rags, one with an eye patch
   over the hole an anti-personnel
mine left. This is November, someone says.
   What will we do when winter comes?

A man who survived a village massacre
    points to the seam stitched

in his cheek. He shows the crusted-over
    slash under his forage cap, a filigree
of pink, new skin. They wore black masks,
    he says. They murdered us in our beds:
Kamal, Zoran, Alma and her baby, Murat
    my grandson, who was only seven.
I crawled into the forest. An UNPROFOR
    truck brought me here where I know

no one. I would hang myself, if not
    for fear of hell, but can it be worse
than this? Then this is inescapable:
    the weather turning bitter, a flood
of refugees, falling shells the trees
    can't hold, death in too many guises
to avoid. A regiment of pigeons bursts
    from upper girders, quarreling

as they circle and resettle, everyone
    skittish. Just down the road,
past burned-out Saabs and Yugos,
    the Povitica bakery may reopen.
The site's a shrine of emaciated flowers
    and snapshots for twenty-two civilians
in line for bread last May shredded
    by a mortar. Later, a local cellist

played Albinoni's "Adagio in G Minor"
    twenty-two days on the sidewalk
to commemorate the dead, the piece based
    on a single sheet of music found
on a Dresden street after the firebombing.
    Casualties are so commonplace
no one sees them anymore: Thadamir Sulentic,
    12 and legless, his parents ten meters

closer to the artillery explosion, tells
    an aid worker that to cry from terror
is worse than to cry from sadness. He dreams,
    he says, of golden wings and flying,
but not like angels, no—like a mythological
    bird of prey with talons and teeth
to rip out the killers' hearts and
    kill them all until there's peace.

Blues, For Bill

How fitting that he should come back as blues,
the whole panoply from indigo to ultramarine
on two wings, as cows lumbered up the swale

to a hilltop pasture, the sun sunk behind the now
truly named Blue Ridge, the world in deepening
shadow. How perfect that he should come back

as a butterfly, and yet, given his love of words
and where they come from, how apt it should be
in the blues of a Red-spotted Purple, southerly

conspecific to the White Admiral she might find
in the city where they lived. This is her first summer
in this state; this is the first blue butterfly she's

ever seen. She is wearing blue jeans. She stands
just beyond the shade of a tall walnut tree,
watching day fade. Except for the cattle, it is

utterly quiet. The butterfly alights on her right hip
and stays, its quivering subsiding slowly to calm.
She could touch it, but doesn't. The Incas believed

warriors fallen in battle visit loved ones left behind
as butterflies, she learns later. She knows very little
of this then. She still doesn't know what happened

to his ashes, his cookbooks and jazz, the last message
she left. She knows where his books went, who took
in Velcro. To satisfy him she learned the difference

between twilight and dusk. She tries not to budge,
to breathe as lightly as she can. With nightfall, he lifts
off. She knows how lucky she is. How lucky she was.

JULIE BRUCK

This Morning, After an Execution at San Quentin

My husband said he felt human again
after days of stomach flu, made himself French toast,
                    then lay down again to be sure.

I took our daughter to the zoo,
where she stood on small flowered legs, transfixed by the drone
                    of the Howler monkey,
            a sound more retch than howl.

Singing monkey, my girl says.
She is well-rested. We all are. As we slept, cold spring air arrived,
                    blown from the Bay where San Quentin
                    casts its sharp light.

Tonight, my girl will tell her father
(a man restored, even grateful, for a day or so), about what she
                    saw in the raised cage.
            Monkey singing, she will tell him,

And later, tell every corner of her cool dark room,
until the crib springs ease because she's run out of joy,
                    and fallen asleep on her knees.

JAN CLAUSEN

From a Glass House

Percussion at bedtime!
A fist-sized rock, well-aimed,
wrecked two windowpanes
and missile-cruised my living room,
bestowing transparent sharpness;
ricocheted; reposed
on a walnut bookshelf
thick with history
(the Black Jacobins, class war
in ancient Greece).
Glittering quills adorned
a potted palm.

The projectile
excited scrutiny:
its mongrel shape lopsided—
round, then sharp;
its colors muddy, mixed;
its grizzled surface
something one might climb
with pitons, rope, and nerve.
No casual pebble
from our Brooklyn street
but micro-intifada's
meditated instrument.

The cops, invited, came
and shook their heads
at damaged plaster,
angle of descent.
"He shoulda been a pitcher,"
said the paler of the pair

to the miscegenated owners
of such fragile property.

He. But I know a woman
steeped in shattering.
("Mary would have swung
that bottle at my head
if the windshield
hadn't stopped her.")
I, too, have guessed the joy
of smashing vitreous taboo,
annihilating structure,
letting outside weather in.

Last week the children came
for Halloween. Some were poor:
dark, rough boys
without disguise or parents,
giddy, jostling.
Sometimes I feel a little nervous
answering my door.

Now I stand on the porch
where my enemy must have stood
to hurl her bitter tool,
his rude machine.
Why do I like to weigh it
in my hand?—
a stone with the mug
of a washed-up pugilist.
A humble emissary from
the Law of Gravity.

All day we keep dissecting
the physics of the thing.

For My Unnamed Brother (1943–1943)

I was left out
I was chosen second & then left out
I was left
handed I was left
to fend for myself I
was the second in
command I was the second
in line I came
without directions

*

I want the
milk   I want my
first pick   I want
choice & all its implications   there was a

residue of
scar
between us   it chafed
when we rubbed our
chests together

*

           hello, brother, hello?
hello in there, brother, can you
hear me?   it's a long
tunnel to the grave   speak, speak

weary saint, you were my
first god   I was rapt in your
coming
      mother better
eat her vegetables, she better chew chew
chew

what's bitter between us

*

               I want the

milk, I need it for my
teeth   they're
soft, the gums
bleed   there's evidence

on my toothbrush   I got the
second draft   I need calcium
to make up   I

got a job
     & left
I don't know where you're
buried

*

what do you
need?   what will make you
happy?   what do you
want?   the dead
do have mouths &
appetites   suck it
up   there's plenty in the ice
box   more
where that came from

*

              if somebody
asked me what's
next, I wouldn't
know   I took my hands off
like something
hot or fragile or in
pain   I was
aghast at suffering, how you can feed
& feed it
       & it's never
full

*

             there's a separation
between us, a suppuration, there's just the
space of an idea   I don't know what's
missing   it's a blind
spot   sometimes my left eye
focuses & it's like looking at
both of us through a
window

*

      I'm telling you the
facts of life, for
you haven't been told
yet   you're in your late
50's, you're dis-
eased or disinterested, a
queer unable to
come out of the casket   o.k.

*

you live this
life & I'll live the
next   she only has enough milk for
one baby   I'll go
around this
time   you come the
next   that time you'll have a
better mother   I
promise you that

Leavings

My brother went to Indiana and came back dead.
From the ice-blasted plains he wrote me one letter.
"Class is hard. My roommate smells like a horse.
I have a job as a security guard. A car would be good.
Send curry." My mother sent the chicken dripping
onto plastic in a box; the car came later for five hundred
dollars from an Indiana friend. Oh my brother, he didn't know
the food would be so flat, and the roads, those belly-
of-the-country roads, he didn't know they could be so black,
the lines vanishing before headlights and fog, shadows
humping for miles along a lone car, straddling the mind like light
bouncing off a highway in the sun, the mirages of mountains, deer
that morphed into facets and knives in the sunset of a windshield.
My brother went to Indiana. They sent us his shirt.
There is a golden badge on the shoulder,
an empty breast pocket, and it is crisp, as he kept things.

EUGENE DUBNOV

Is There a Print

Is there
a print
left by the toes
upon the umbered surface
of the stone
on which the farmer's daughter
stepped in the springtime
to reach
the top of the fence
between the cornfield
and the water meadow—
I would like to have inquired
whether somewhere
there does not remain
the trace
of her delicate foot,
if the memory lingers
of her way of walking
or of her running,
or of her body's resting
in the grass by the waterside?
She had drowned, they told me,
last autumn, swimming by night in the cold river.

translated from the Russian by John Heath-Stubbs with the author

The Zen of Alice

Alice is pushing 40, her sprawling hips so sprawled that when she
busts out of the White Rabbit's House, Lewis
Carrol has to play handyman, nailing the
door and roof back on.
Every time she tries to sneak away through the garden, the path
flings her back, like a treadmill going too fast. She crushes
gardenias with her butt, the Looking-Glass
hyacinth nothing but torn petals. It is said that Lewis lost
interest as soon as Alice got breasts. The White Queen fed her
jam which became her distraction over the years. The
King of Hearts is the only king still without a mustache—and
Lewis, Alice fears, is now writing adventures for him.
Men her size or age are nowhere to be found.
Never mind a girlfriend to hang with
or a shopping mall where she can buy face creams or
perfume. Even her Dodo bird is only
quasi-hers. He flits away easily and lately
returns with a mouse in his jaw.
Stranger-than-usual things have been happening. Alice's
Twiddledee and Tweedledum tattoos disappear as a field of
umbrellas changes into a field of bowling balls that
veer with malice towards passersby.
What kind of a wonderland has this become? wonders Alice
    whose chest
x-ray is nothing more than a bowl of
Yorkshire pudding, whose
zits have long faded into zilch.

The Monsters at the Edge of the World

for my wife, Katherine

The film of your brain
is a map drawn by conquerors
flying the banner of exploration
and misnaming all the islands,
yet we sail through the clouds
swirling in this hemisphere,
navigate rivers of silver
till we find the white slash
circled in red that tells us
stroke, hemorrhage,
as if saying that monsters dwell here
at the edge of the world, and nowhere
do we see the lake where one night
we drifted in a wooden boat
with a bottle of wine
and dangled sparklers
over the starry water.

Inheritance of Waterfalls and Sharks

for my son, Klemente Gilbert-Espada

In 1898, with the infantry from Illinois,
the boy who would become the poet Sandburg
rowed his captain's Saint Bernard ashore
at Guánica, and watched as the captain
lobbed cubes of steak at the canine snout.
The troops speared mangos with bayonets
like many suns thudding with shredded yellow flesh
to earth. General Miles, who chained Geronimo
for the photograph in sepia of the last renegade,
promised Puerto Rico the *blessings of enlightened civilization.*
Private Sandburg marched, peeking at a book
nested in his palm for the words of Shakespeare.

Dazed in blue wool and sunstroke, they stumbled up the mountain
to Utuado, learned the war was over, and stumbled away.
Sandburg never met Great-great-grand-uncle Don Luis,
who wore a linen suit that would not wrinkle,
read with baritone clarity scenes from *Hamlet*
house to house for meals of rice and beans,
the Danish prince and his soliloquy—*ser o no ser*—
saluted by rum, the ghost of Hamlet's father wandering
through the ceremonial ball courts of the Taíno.

In Caguas or Cayey Don Luis
was the reader at the cigar factory,
newspapers in the morning,
Cervantes or Marx in the afternoon,
rocking with the whirl of an unseen sword
when Quijote roared his challenge to giants,
weaving the tendrils of his beard when he spoke
of labor and capital, as the *tabaqueros*
rolled leaves of tobacco to smolder in distant mouths.

Maybe he was the man of the same name
who published a sonnet in the magazine of browning leaves
from the year of the Great War and the cigar strike.
He disappeared; there were rumors of Brazil,
inciting cane cutters or marrying the patrón's daughter,
maybe both, but always the reader,
whipping Quijote's sword overhead.

Another century, and still the warships scavenge
Puerto Rico's beaches with wet snouts. For practice,
Navy guns hail shells coated with uranium over Vieques
like a boy spinning his first curveball;
to the fisherman on the shore, the lung is a net
and the tumor is a creature with his own face, gasping.

This family has no will, no house, no farm, no island.
But today the great-great-great-grand-nephew of Don Luis,
not yet ten, named for a jailed poet and fathered by another poet,
in a church of the Puritan colony called Massachusetts,
wobbles on a crate and grabs the podium
to read his poem about El Yunque waterfalls
and Achill basking sharks, and shouts:
I love this.

En la calle San Sebastián

Viejo San Juan, Puerto Rico, 1998

Here in a bar on the street of the saint
en la calle San Sebastián,
a dancer in white with a red red scarf
en la calle San Sebastián,
calls to the gods who were freed by slaves
en la calle San Sebastián,
and his bronze face is a lantern of sweat
en la calle San Sebastián,
and hands smack congas like flies in the field
en la calle San Sebastián,
and remember the beat of packing crates
en la calle San Sebastián,
from the days when overseers banished the drum
en la calle San Sebastián,
and trumpets screech like parrots of gold
en la calle San Sebastián,
trumpets that herald the end of the war
en la calle San Sebastián,
as soldiers toss rifles on cobblestone
en la calle San Sebastián,
and the saint himself snaps an arrow in half
en la calle San Sebastián,
then lost grandfathers and fathers appear
en la calle San Sebastián,
fingers tugging my steel-wool beard
en la calle San Sebastián,
whispering *Your beard is gray*
en la calle San Sebastián,
spilling their rum across the table
en la calle San Sebastián,
till cousins lead them away to bed
en la calle San Sebastián,
and the dancer in white with a face of bronze
en la calle San Sebastián,

shakes rain from his hair like the god of storms
en la calle San Sebastián,
and sings for the blood that drums in the chest
en la calle San Sebastián,
and praises the blood that beats in the hands
en la calle San Sebastián,
en la calle San Sebastián.

Run Away, My Pale Love

This was just before my thirtieth birthday. I was in graduate school, of all places. I had no idea why. None of us did. We were extremely well-spoken rubber duckies. You could push us in any one direction, and we would flounder on forever. Sometimes, in the drowsy winter hallways, my conscience would rear up and remind me I was dumb with luck. Other times, I wished they'd turn the whole place into a homeless shelter.

But the day I'm talking about was early spring. The callery pears were in blossom, thousands of tiny white camisoles. I was out in front of the Comp Lit compound with Legget, watching the undergrads. We were vaguely aware of the distinctions between them. Mostly, they were just tan calves drifting past.

A woman entered my field of vision from the right. She had the plumpest cheeks I'd ever seen. Her eyes were pinched at the corners, and blue patches stood out below them. She looked as if she hadn't slept in a year. Every other woman I could think of seemed stingy and coarse and obvious by comparison. She waved timidly at Legget.

"You like that, do you?" he said.

"Who is she?"

"She's in my French class." Legget stubbed out his cigarette. "Polish, I think."

"What's her name?"

"Don't know," Legget said. "She doesn't say much."

For the next week, I walked around babbling about The Polish Woman. "You know me," I said. "I don't gawk. I'm not a gawker." This was more or less true. Somewhere in the mid-twenties it dawned on me that female beauty didn't require any encouragement from me. Female beauty was doing just fine on its own. But I couldn't get this woman out of my head.

Legget diagnosed sexual infatuation.

"Can't I just have an aesthetic experience?" I said. "Like spotting a rare species, a species you might see once and never again, for the rest of your life?"

"Spare me," Legget said.

Two months later, in the computer lab, a woman in a white blouse swept into the seat next to mine. "Is it all right?" she said. Her accent was excruciating: the burred diphthongs of Russian, the sulky lilt of French. My heart did a little arpeggio.

"You're Polish," I said.

She turned, and there was her face again. Her lips drew together, as if stung by some impending calamity. "Yah. How do you know?"

I explained about Legget. She nodded slowly.

"Do you like Kosinski?" I said.

"Oh yah!" she said. "Have you read *Painted Bird*?"

"Sure," I said. "Wow. It's hard to find anyone who's read Kosinski." This was true. I myself, for instance, had not read Kosinski, though I'd heard he was quite good. "What a writer!" I said. "What sentences!" On and on I went until, finally, at a loss for what to say next, I asked for her phone number.

She looked at me for a few seconds—I was in my teaching uniform, a rumpled white button-down and khakis—then wrote her name on a piece of paper: *Basha*.

"I don't do this normally," I said. "But, I mean, I really love Kosinski."

And then she was standing on the median of Summit Avenue, lit up inside a beige windbreaker. She looked elegant and chimerical: the head of a lioness, the body of a swan. At dinner, I choked on my chicken korma. That was just for starters. I got lost on the way to the theater. I misplaced my wallet, and had to race home to get cash. We were twenty minutes late to the movie—a British drawing-room melodrama—and sat in the darkened theater trying to figure out who was doomed and who fated. I spent most of the time smelling Basha, glancing at her profile, my fingers greasy with popcorn.

The amateur psychologists in the crowd will perhaps sense the significance of the lost wallet: *The subject subconsciously enacts a fantasy in which he is stripped of his identity through a powerful, exotic love.*

To which I would respond: *Doy hickey.*

I was ravenous for an affair so grandiose as to obliterate my life. Most every relationship I'd formed in the past five years had gone south: romantic entanglements, friendships, professional alliances. One friend referred to me as a train wreck. Another suggested "emotional atom bomb" as perhaps closer to the mark. The ones I couldn't scare away, I managed to drive off over some perceived slight. I was the world's welterweight champion of the silent feud. I didn't see it that way, of course. People just kept letting me down. It never occurred to me that I sought out rejection, engineered the drama of fresh grievances to distract me from older, stale forms of grief.

But that's not the story I'm telling now. No one—except those paid to listen—really wants to hear your musty songs of self-contempt. What we want is the glib aria of disastrous love, which is, finally, the purest expression of self-contempt.

Her full name was Basha Sabina Olszewska. She pronounced her last name beautifully: *Olshevska.* It meant something like a birch tree, she said. I thought of Frost: the pale trunk, the quick fire. She came from Katowice, an industrial city in the west of Poland. She hoped to become a translator. English was her fifth language.

She had a sense of humor as well. Imagine. She told me a story about dining with the Dean of Students at a welcoming banquet for exchange students. "They brought him steak," she said. "I couldn't believe the size. It was like a car tire. Everyone was quiet for a second, and just at that minute I turned to him and said: 'You have such huge meat!' "

This story thrilled me—its slapstick reference to the male part. Basha knew what a cock was! She understood the great harmless joke that all cocks come to in the end. And this idea, however improbably, led to the idea that she might touch my cock.

We were eating at my place. She was sitting there at my table, daintily cutting her chicken. I told stories about my life that suggested—far less subtly than I supposed—what a terrific guy I was. I cleared her plate and took it to the sink. Wasn't I the disarmingly liberated bachelor type? She stood. I stepped in front of her and let my face fall forward. She executed a brisk little side-step. My lips smeared the side of her cheek. A pine cone fell from the tree outside, striking the roof with a soft thud, as if to close the subject.

Later, standing outside her dorm, I said: "Will I ever get to kiss you?"

Her lips pursed, like a waiter who is out of the most popular item on the menu. The light fell across her in frets. "Such an American question!" She told me about some Finnish jerk she'd fallen for first term. And now she was returning to Poland and felt too vulnerable—the word seemed to swirl around her tongue—to get involved.

To which I wanted to say: Involved? Who needs *involved*?

This was one of the advantages of age. I'd been rejected enough times to understand that prudence meant little in the face of sustained negotiation. Virtue was a better guide, all things considered. You could maybe depend on virtue. But a guy like me, with my wonderful rage, my American case of Manifest Destiny, I wasn't about to back down from a little prudence. "Sure," I said. "I understand. I hope we can still hang out."

Basha was so relieved at my grace, she gave herself to me. She needed the help of a large bottle of inexpensive sauvignon blanc, which disappeared down her throat, cup by cup, while I watched in cautious rapture. It seemed terribly important that I do nothing to startle her. Slowly, perceptibly, my kitchen grew warm with the promise of contact. I can't recall a word that passed between us. There was only the wine, my silence, her mouth fixing to the rim of her cup, the slight, glottal pull of her underlip against and away from its surface, her white throat reaching up, descending.

We kissed, and she smiled, her lips turning back on themselves. Her teeth were faintly discolored, as if she'd had a quick bite of ashes. I had never seen the classic Slavic facial structure at such close quarters. When she laughed, her cheeks rose with the strange, graceful bulk of glaciers and her eyes became Mongol slashes. Frowning, her mouth took on the milky petulance of a Tartar princess. Even at rest, impassive, her face expressed the severe emotions I associated with true love, which I had always known to be exquisite and doomed and slightly stylized.

I felt the pleasing thickness of her, damp beneath her garments. We were on my mattress, yanking off clothes. She had narrow shoulders, tiny budded breasts. Her arms and belly were robed in baby fat.

We made love, or fucked, did that thing where our center parts fit and unfit, a half dozen times, in panicky sessions, ten minutes or so, until she cried out *Tak! Tak!* then fell still. She consented to my movements with her body and spoke only once, toward dawn, saying, as my hand brushed up her thigh, "I am having so wet." I knew then—at that exact moment—Basha had been sent to rescue me from the dull plight of my life.

This, it would turn out, is the main thing we had in common: a susceptibility to the brassy escapism of myth.

I saw her across the street, her arms poking out of a red dress with white polka dots, the fabric tight around her bum. She came to me and kissed me, and I could smell the rot of her mouth. And the rot of her mouth turned me on! (Is there nothing the early days of love won't fetishize?)

We went to the mall, to buy last-minute gifts. Basha circled the pavilion, fretting over a belt, a bottle of lotion, blushing at the inquiries of the sales staff. She was a nervous shopper, which I took to be a mark of her unfamiliarity with the ritual. I had all sorts of crappy ideas rattling around my head about life in Poland. I knew, vaguely, that the Poles had broken from the Soviet Bloc. But I still imagined a lumpen gulag: endless lines, bare shelves, faces like potatoes in kerchiefs. And my poor Basha trapped amid this needy vulgarity! I stood behind her and called out to the clerks: *One of those! Make it two! Why not? Do you have this in black?*

Our relationship was filed under *dalliance,* which allowed us to write one another without much pressure. Basha was an excellent correspondent. She made it a point to send me sexy photos of herself. My favorite showed her leaning toward the camera, kissing at a cigarette, mascara smeared, hair tousled—a Bond girl at the end of a long vodka party.

That summer, I got stoned, sat on my porch, tried to figure out where everyone had gone. Across the street, guys with whistles were running a girls' soccer camp, which I could watch if I wasn't too obvious. The girls were sweet and clumsy. They lacked the essentials of the sport—the ability to steal and confront and tackle—but their legs enjoyed flirting with these ideas. I was supposed to be writing a dissertation.

My answering machine was the enemy. Often, returning from the grocery store, or the Greek diner where I took suppers, I gazed at the red zero flashing smugly and punched the machine. Then, one day, there was a message.

Hayizmeimeezyucullme.

When I called her back, Basha wanted to know, immediately, if she would ever see me again. "I made a breakup with my boyfriend," she said.

"What boyfriend?"

"It doesn't matter," she said. "I have my vacations at end of August."

At the airport in Warsaw, she came running, her eyes blurry hazel, a skirt shaping her hips, and she was far too beautiful for me, my sharp face and chickeny bones. I felt (as I often feel) a dramatic error in the accounting, though she pressed herself to me and made me feel, thereby, in the midst of that lousy airport, with its plastic counters and vague feculence, different from myself, heroic.

We found a cheap hotel and signed in as man and wife. Basha did the talking, while the concierge squinted at her.

"She thinks I am a whore," Basha said in the elevator. She smiled, her gums like a second, wetter smile. "Maybe I am a whore." She shut the door to our room, and tore the button off my pants. I'd seen this sort of thing, in films hoping to suggest reckless passion. But this was the first time I'd been inside the animal experience, so famished for physical love as to overleap the gooey crescendo of intimacy. We never even got our shirts off.

Basha wanted nothing to do with clitoral stimulation, tricky positioning, languorous gazes. Put it in, was her agenda. Let the flesh speak. Her face went rubbery. She took on the aspect of a madwoman plucked from one of Hogarth's Bedlam prints, ready to tear her hair, throw shit, which pleased me, as did her internal muscles, which yielded in rings of contraction. Sun from the window lit a glaze of nervous perspiration on her small white breasts. Her hips rocked.

"Make big come," she said. "Make big come in my pussy."

"Tell me—"

"Now. Now-now-*now.*"

Afterward, her body looked like something tossed ashore.

Basha reached down and took hold of me: "You have huge meat."

I laughed.

"Really," she said.

"I'm pretty sure I have normal meat," I said.

"No," she said. "I remember the first time we were together, when I first saw, thinking this."

I studied her expression for some sign of caginess. But caginess was not her style. She didn't speak about the particulars of sex in the same way an American woman might. And she appeared quite serious in her assessment, as if my size were a matter she had considered privately.

My ego flew in wild circles overhead. Is there nothing man desires more than to be regaled about his own huge meat?

Basha didn't remember her father, who had died when she was two years old. He was no more than a blurry figure in photographs, with her tiny arrow of a nose and tangled teeth. Her first love—her only great love, from what I could tell—was her stepfather, Tomas, a gentle mathematician who had worshipped Basha's mother.

"What happened to him?" I said.

"He died when I was eight," she said. "Returning from a conference in Germany. There was snow on the road."

"My God," I said. "I'm so sorry."

I reached for Basha, but she slipped to the side of the bed and sat up, regarding me curiously. "Don't be sorry. I barely remember."

In Krakow, we went to see the palace, but it was closed for repairs, so we walked to the other end of the plaza. The tourist bureau had organized a folk dancing festival, surly teenagers spinning in peasant garb. Basha herself wore a summer dress, loose around the legs, and open-toed sandals. I thought about all the girls in their summer dresses, and tried to understand why I cared only to look at Basha.

We made love in our muggy pension room, lathered one another in the shower, then returned to the plaza to feel the breeze on our limbs, which were sore in secret places, to watch the stars against the drape of night and browse the stalls of painted eggs and cigarette cases. The cafés were open, the tabletops lit by bouncing candles.

My own tranquility astounded me.

"What do you think about?" Basha said.

"Night," I said. "A beautiful night like this."

She squeezed my hand and leaned in for a kiss. Her eyes were deep green and perfectly serious. In a soft, almost embarrassed voice, she said: "I want to come to America to make a life with you, David." Her hands were trembling. Her breathing was ragged. This was all terribly real. I had to remind myself.

"Yes?" she whispered. "What do you think about it?"

Hadn't I come to Poland in the hopes of just such a plea? Don't we all, in the private kingdom of our desires, dream about such pleas? And yet, there was something deflating about the declaration. Without warning, in one sentence, Basha had called an end to the hunt, laid herself before me, forced me to make good on the promises of my extravagant furious charm. I felt my heart chop.

We were ideally suited to the long-distance relationship, with its twisted calculus of wish fantasy and deprivation. We wrote long epistles full of desire and ardent grief. We perfected the art of nostalgia: extracting the finer moments from the tangle of actual experience, burnishing them with new longing. We took the inconvenience of our love as the proof of its profundity.

And so, Christmas in Poland. Katowice struck me as suitably impoverished. Men selling carp on the corners, slashing the fish until blood soaked their aprons, while the wives peddled the shiny roe. Everyone looked glum and underdressed; the sidewalks ran off into mud.

Basha lived with her mother, but they were both at work. She'd left me the key to the apartment. Her building was part of a massive Soviet-style *panelak,* crinkled like a fan, five stories of concrete smeared with soot, stairwells sharp with piss. Her room was the size of a cell: a single bed, a dresser, a desk with my letters neatly stacked in one corner. Over the bed, she'd taped a picture of us kissing on a street corner in Krakow. I'd taken the photo myself, holding the camera with one hand while hauling her into an embrace. The white pelt of Basha's cheek was draped across the frame, her eyes closed, her mouth thrown toward the kiss. The photo was blurred: as if the action captured had been terribly swift, or the moment dreamed. Outside, snow fell like confetti, dissolving on the pavement. Every time I heard the tock of a woman's shoes, my body tensed.

Basha burst into the apartment finally, out of breath, her eyes glassy. I experienced the brief paralysis of gratification. *You mean this is actually mine?* Her hands slipped beneath my sweater. Her minty tongue touched mine. Basha hauled me into her room. The smell of her rose up, a sweet bacterial tang. She let out a luxurious sigh as I slid into her. So much drama! It was like leaping onto Broadway cock-first.

And later, scrubbed and pink-eared, I sat at the Olszewskas' dining room table, gorged on rice laced with cumin and slivers of sautéed liver. Mamu appeared, flushed from the cold (and, it would turn out, a good deal of wine). She was a handsome woman, wide cheeks and a plucked mouth. Basha's face bloomed. It was clear at once that they were deeply in love, as mothers and daughters sometimes grow to be, without the interfering needs of men.

I stood, and Mamu looked me over. I could see Basha watching us, the slowing of her breath. Mamu shook my hand and announced, in her wobbly English, that she was delighted to meet me. Then she pulled me into a sloppy hug, and Basha laughed and pulled me back to her side, scolding Mamu in Polish, a language that seemed to me always, in the mouths of the Olszewska women, a volley of quick and playful whispers.

What did I have to do? Stand there and look pretty. This was the secret dividend of loving a woman from a foreign country: very little was required of me.

"We will have wodka," Mamu said.

"*Vodka*," Basha said.

"*Vodka*," Mamu corrected herself elaborately.

Yes! Vodka with bitter tonic and lemon wedges, drunk from tall glasses. And later, in Mamu's room, plum brandy from snifters. The three of us were huddled at the foot of her bed; there was no other place to sit. Her room accommodated a single bed, a bookshelf, a small dresser for clothes.

Mamu was one of those smokers whose motions are so calm and practiced, so assumed, that the act becomes an extension of their personality. She preferred a brand called Petit Coeurs, whose box was decorated in tiny gray hearts. The cigarettes themselves were as slender as lollipop sticks. Mamu could kill one in six draws, though often she let them burn down untended, the ashes making elegant snakes. She seemed to enjoy the option of smoking as much as the act.

Basha and I took the tram to the central plaza, with its smooth new cobblestone and stately, gabled buildings, refurbished with foreign money and painted in cake-frosting colors. These housed clubs and restaurants and clothing shops, for tourists, of course, but also for the emerging class of strivers represented by Basha and her friends, who had learned the first lesson of the bourgeoisie: that the acquisition of wealth required, to some mysterious degree, the appearance of wealth.

We visited a few clubs, smoky places full of old pop songs and young people trying hard to acquire the defensive irony of American culture. This made me sad. But liquor helped soften my sadness, helped me occupy a little more gracefully my role as Basha's exuberant Americanski. We wound up in some hotel lounge. Basha was there, next to me, laughing. The other women, dour and beautiful, watched me. I downed shot after shot and proposed toasts in mangled French and serenaded Basha with a fair rendition of Elvis Presley. Some fellow pulled a glass pipe from his pocket. "Hash," he said. "Hashish." I smoked some of that, too. Sure. I was the star. The star drinks. The star smokes.

Then we were outside, on the stumbling cobblestone, under the splotchy moon. Basha folded herself into me. Everything about her seemed perfect just then: her cheeks, the way her mouth smooshed vowels, her new decadence, her pale body. She was emotionally inobvious. That was true. But wasn't that just part of the mystery? Wasn't that, in some sense, the entire point?

That we made love, I recognized only by the feeling of my lower body, a wet, suctiony joy. Most nights, I would have curled around her, kissing the skin between her shoulder blades, my low arm going slowly numb beneath her. But the bed didn't seem entirely solid, seemed more in the nature of an ocean. Salt rose in my throat, and I staggered to the bathroom. My body heaved and gasped. I suspected—as do all unpracticed drinkers—that I would never feel right again. Far above, I could see the racks of emollients, Basha's cherished blow-dryer, pantyhose laid like molted skin across the radiator, a calliope of homely bras.

There was a tap on the door. Basha. Basha come to rescue her lover.

I struggled to my feet and opened the door. Mamu stood in her robe, blinking. I was naked. My penis dangled. The sweetness of her daughter's sex, like flesh that has been perfumed and licked, rose into the air between us. I wanted to duck behind the door, but in that moment such an action seemed to constitute an accusation.

"You are sick?" Mamu said. She was careful not to let her gaze drop below my chest.

"I drank too much," I said. "Wodka." I pantomimed taking a shot, and in this motion, as my arm rose to my mouth, my fingers flipped toward my lips, I became acutely aware of my cock, rising up, settling back.

"You would like tea?" Mamu said.

"Oh no." I laid a palm on my stomach. Mamu glanced down, not entirely understanding the gesture, and her eyes settled there for a moment, not even a moment, a charged little half moment.

How long had it been since Mamu had looked upon the chicken-necked vanity of a man's sex? She had buried two husbands, and, by Basha's account, no longer considered the idea. But Basha did not yet understand what a stubborn customer the body is. The heart may turn the lights out. The body never closes for business.

"No tea?" she said.

"No, thank you."

"Okay," Mamu whispered. She stepped back into the hallway and turned; her robe traced the soft square of her hips. She had the same body as Basha, after all, only dragged by time, by the tolls of motherhood.

"Sorry for waking you up," I said.

She turned back to me, and her face emerged from the shadows so abruptly it was as if she had leapt toward me. I ducked behind the door. This was not a conscious act. My body, drunken and shy, simply reacted. And yet the expression which settled onto Mamu's face then seemed unutterably sad. Her teeth carved out a tiny failed smile. "It doesn't matter to me," she said.

Mamu spent the day before my departure preparing borscht. The windows fogged with a bouquet of onions fried in chicken fat, celery, carrots, peppers, the subtle acrid undercurrent of beets. I'd never eaten borscht. That was the joke. From time to time, I shambled to the kitchen to fetch tea from the porcelain kettle that stood, perpetually steeping, on the narrow ledge between oven and sink. I paused to watch Mamu core the eyes out of a potato.

"She is sad," Mamu said quietly. "Are you sad?"

"Yes," I said.

She raised her hands, as if to make a gesture, and her fingertips came to rest on my cheekbone. I could smell the dirt and onions on her hands, which were beautiful, pink and swollen, the backs laced with delicate veins. "Yes. Sad."

After dinner, we drank vodka. Mamu put some folk music on the record player, and Basha attempted to teach me the rudiments of a polka. Then Mamu rose from her seat, handed me her softer body, which moved with a surprising buoyancy.

And later, piled into her room, Mamu pulled a silver punch bowl from beneath her bed, filled with family photos. There she was, thirty years ago, on a youth brigade outing, a pretty, stylish teenager in a uniform and a beret. She looked at me as I looked at the photos, leaned against my shoulder. Her face sang out the same caption again and again: *This is me, young and beautiful!*

There were other photos she wanted me to see: Basha looking darling in a white pinafore, nestled on the lap of her stepfather, fending off sleep with a gummy smile. Mamu set her hand on my thigh. She leaned toward me. For a moment, I thought she would kiss me, that her red, smoky mouth would seek mine. But I was missing it. The person she was reaching for was Basha. The photos fell from her lap, her youth, her motherhood, her daughter, the men she loved, all tumbling onto the rug, face up, face down, the bowl used for storing them showing streaks of tarnish under the amber light.

Basha clambered off the bed and went down onto her forearms, pushing her backside into the air. She was quite drunk.

"Do you like the way I look like this?"

It took me a moment to gather my voice, and Basha laughed, as we should wish all women to laugh, at the fallacy of their depravity, at the idea that anything, in the end, can disgust them. "I want anal love," she said, making the word sound French and exquisite.

Is it cruel for me to repeat her words like this? Should I lie, make them somehow prettier, more poetic? But this is what she said. This is the form her desire took at that moment. Or perhaps, less flatteringly, she intuited my need for a memorable degradation, some form of going-away present.

"Are you sure?" I said.

"Put some jelly." Basha sucked in a little breath and pushed back. The heel of her palms pressed down, and her arms tensed. I braced my heel against the radiator. The knuckles of her spine buckled softly. Her face was pressed to the rug, and her eyes were closed, and she was smiling.

I could hear Mamu in the bathroom, making her ablutions before bed.

"We should stop," I said.

Basha shook her head: *No, it feels good, but it hurts, let's keep trying.*

There were other women around, more suitable, in baggy sweaters and glasses much like mine, their clocks fizzing away. But I was in no shape to cooperate with them. The last thing I wanted was a woman who actually understood me. Once back in the States, that is, face to face with the prospect of a reasonable adulthood, I fell back under the aegis of my own bloated heroism. I knew I was being played. But that, too, is a part of love. I missed

Basha. I missed her Old World manners, which made me feel debonair. I missed Mamu's greasy borscht and her confused longing. I missed their warm little apartment, where I was always the center of attention.

Katowice was made new by May. The buildings, ash-streaked and rotten in winter, bloomed with mongrel hyacinth. Sun baked the mud to dirt. Shirts fluttered brightly on laundry lines, and kids kicked soccer balls in the courtyards, and couples in long shadows strolled the plaza at dusk. With the windows thrown open, the breeze carried the fragrance of broiled chicken and baked sesame seeds, the sweet reek of garbage.

And the women! The women of Katowice unpeeled themselves, plum-titted, translucent, with cheeks a mile square and big sleepy asses, teenagers in sullen halter-tops, business molls slotted into rayon suits, college students spilling from green miniskirts, young mommies pushing strollers. And the girls of the meat shops, whose flanks and chops sweated in glass cases, whose beauty hid beneath tiers of acne, who handled the sweet, smoky kielbasa as if handling thick lovers—brisk, worldly imitations of sex!

Each morning, Basha and Mamu bustled off to work, while I got up and pretended to write. I was hard at work on what was— to my knowledge—the longest outline in academic history: 471 pages, not counting footnotes. At noon, I fixed myself a breakfast of eggs, sugar-cured bacon, rolls pan-fried in the fat. Then I settled down for a nap, listening to the yips of the kids on the playground below. It was all quite bohemian. I smoked Walet cigarettes, at eighty-five groszy a pack, which tasted of cloves and dung.

In the evenings, I talked literature with Mamu. She'd studied philology at the university, and devoured the Western Canon. *Die Blechtrummel* was an after-dinner mint to her. I bounced a few of my ideas her way, and they came back deboned and neatly skinned. Basha preferred TV, which consisted, in large part, of American sitcoms dubbed into Polish by a single droning monotone.

Aside from sexual congress, during which her mind and body seemed open to the fluctuations of experience, she remained determinedly opaque. She was not dumb, or shallow. She had mastered five languages and spoke each of them beautifully.

There seemed no sound her tongue couldn't make. She simply mistrusted the depth of her feelings.

But even our glorious sex life wilted under the rigor of permanence. Basha kept me on what the behavioralists would recognize as a variable reinforcement schedule. She wanted to be cuddled, fawned over, stroked like a child. If I pushed for more, she claimed to be sore, or tired. I couldn't figure this out. Where had the wanton accomplice of our early days gone? Once a week or so, I staged a blowout, on some despicable pretext, so as to storm out of the apartment, valiant and misunderstood, and wander the weedy banks of the Valia River, whose slick tides were the color of venous blood; so as to return to the balm of her negligent love, which was for me like floating in a warm sea.

Toward the end of July, an old professor, who had known me in a steadier time, tracked me down. He needed a lecturer for fall. The job itself was no great shakes. But his intention was clear. He was offering me reentry. A decent paycheck. Enough respect to take another pass at my dissertation. "What are you doing over there anyway?" he said.

Basha remained unconvinced. "You won't leave," she said. "You love me too much." She refused to imagine that I had another life, beyond her beauty, thick with the troubled symptoms of adulthood.

"You can come to the States," I said. "Like we talked about."

For all her brave claims of a year ago, Basha said nothing about this plan. Instead, we let the weeks drift by, watched the dour sun elongate the days. The cedars shed elegant white scrolls along the aimless paths where we went to eat ice cream.

On the eve of my departure, I took Basha to Katowice's toniest bistro. We ordered coq au vin and tenderloin braised in anisette. I had hoped to take a last stroll on the plaza, but by the end of the meal, Basha's complexion looked like cement. She barely touched her food. Back at home, Mamu prepared her tea and got her to take aspirin and to lie down.

I finished up packing. When I came to bed, Basha was staring out the window, at the torn clouds. Her face was the kind of thing one sees in the classical wing of a museum: beauty as a force of history. Her robe rode up the back of her thighs. I had it in mind that we might make love. That was what my great, quivering cliché of a body had in mind.

I climbed onto the bed and curled around her from behind and nuzzled against her bottom. "It's our last night together," I said.

Basha shook her head.

"Honey," I whispered. "Please."

"Don't," she said softly. "No."

"I just want to love you." I pressed myself against her.

This was the wrong move. I knew that. But I felt, at that moment, as if I had nothing else to fall back on. Our affair—our grand drama of abandonment and reclamation—had run aground. It was time for our bodies to leap to the rescue.

Basha, for all her evasions, was ahead of me there. She understood that the body can only express wishes. It cannot undo facts. "No," she said. "Leave me alone."

What sort of comment was this? *Leave me alone?* We were lovers. This was our last night. I stared at Basha's long, slender legs. Her skin seemed to grow more and more pale, as if she were dissolving into the sheets. But I didn't want her to go yet. My hand reached for the stem of her neck.

Basha began to weep. "Stop," she said. "Don't touch me."

"Does that hurt?" I pressed at the warm cords of muscle. "Am I hurting you?"

Suddenly Basha was kicking at me, the robe riding up until I could see the cleft of her ass, her lovely white halves tensing, the fine hairs and skin darkening to blue in the furrow. I knew what I wanted to do. It was perfectly clear. I grabbed her hips.

Basha's elbow swung back, knocked me in the mouth, and I could taste blood now, a good taste, sweet and full of ruin. Basha wriggled away and got up from the bed. I might have leapt up, pursued her, done God knows what. But I could see, through the frosted glass of the door, Mamu hovering just outside.

"Run away," I said. "That's right, run away."

"You're the one," Basha sobbed. She opened the door and collapsed into her mother, and the two of them stood there for a minute. Then they moved off, like a pair of wounded soldiers, and I heard the door to Mamu's room swing shut.

I waited for my breathing to subside, then went and stood outside the door. I could hear the two of them whispering in soft drifts of Polish. I opened the door, but neither of them bothered to turn. Mamu reached to straighten the compress she had laid along her daughter's brow. Basha whimpered, in the manner of a child struggling toward sleep. She held the hem of Mamu's skirt in her fist. And I understood, now, why Mamu had never resented my presence: she knew Basha would never forsake her, not in the end.

Mamu emerged from Basha's room an hour later. I was in the kitchen, staring at the empty courtyard below. She smiled politely and took a Petit Coeur from the pack stashed in the cupboard. "Maybe you like sandwich for the trip?"

"That's okay," I said.

But already she was reaching into the fridge, removing a hunk of cheese, some kielbasa wrapped in foil, pulling a knife from the magnetized strip above my head. The skin of her hands was like beautiful pink paper.

"She's asleep?"

Mamu nodded.

"Maybe I should sleep on the couch?"

Mamu shrugged. She sliced the kielbasa and the cheese and layered them on the roll. "You have made all your suitcases?"

I nodded. I could feel the swell of my fat lip.

"I guess I might have hurt her," I said. "I was pretty angry. You know, having to leave and all. We're both a little crazy."

Mamu gazed at me. Smoke drifted from her nose. She had known this was coming, after all. Men were people who left; they were not dependable. Their other charms, their money and their words and their cocks, these were only temporary compensations. Her daughter was finally learning this.

Later, there would be another soggy goodbye, lurid with airport hope. And later still, the letters and phone calls, which slipped to hollow, fainter in their promise, until they vanished altogether. Basha was not the sort to cling, not the sort I might dial up in the small hours, with a bit too much wine and night in me, to make sure she was still somehow stuck. There is a point you reach, I mean, when you are just something bad that happened to someone else.

"I'm sorry," I said. "I'm sorry for everything."

But Mamu wasn't angry. It would be no easier for me in the end. And so she came to me, stepped around the table and gathered me into her arms, and I buried my head in her bosom, which smelled of smoke and laundry soap and ten thousand meals, and began to sob, for Basha, for Mamu, for all of us in the suffering of our desires.

JULIE FAY

Young Lovers on My Beach

He's on top of her, barely
moving, at the swimming hole
I've called mine for years.
Here, to be anything but naked
is nearly sacrilegious.
In the quick red canyon
water sears the dusty plain.
My daughter plays,
oblivious to them, delicious
in her two-year skin,
but I can't not look
(and must if I'm to keep
a mother's eye on her).
She delights the minnows
with her toes, plops and squeals
as the woman's thighs rise, gently
fall just so, flex with his in red
volcanic sand coarse as coffee.

Do they really think I don't know
he's pushed their suits aside just enough
to slip inside? I'm annoyed, surprised
at the depth of my resentment.
It's not that I'm a prude
American in France, I go topless
with the best of them, nude
as often as I might
and don't deny them
the deliciousness of summer's air
on bare skin, the water's green deep,
or fern-drip on rocks red as tongues,
singing bugs tuned to their forever coming

(if they'd just get it over with
for heaven's sake and let us all go on!).

Is it that the married sex
I've come to know's
so hurried and sequestered?
Or is it that they say to me
You don't exist. We are the whole
of this pocket paradise and you're no more
than a mote of cottonwood that floats
past us and we don't see?

Days of 1999

One unexceptional bright afternoon
in August, coming from the rose garden
secreted behind the rue Villehardouin,
I thought, fleet, furtive, *If I lived alone
I could stay here*
          and pushed the thought away
as firmly and unlikely as *Might rain
later* because I wanted just to choose
and I had chosen, more than cobblestones
and arbors, more than the benediction
of new loaves' scent blown from the bakery,
the benediction of the late white rose,
more than the blank page of the cloudless sky,
to honor choice, reflecting on it daily
but even as the thought diminished on
a wave of warm bread and the holiday
banter of children with no homework to do
a choice I never made was made for me
in another mind, another country
I thought I had some claim to, which I knew
not at all, as that warm wave let me drift
with no anticipating harbor left.
Spring showers wash the hidden rose garden;
an evening's bread is rising in an oven:
the afternoon's word resonates *alone*
as a sky, mother-and-fatherless
in its gray and quotidian distress
blurts the repeated questions of the rain.

The Closet

Whether in chrome surgery
or gymnasium toilet—
everyone is expelled
bloody and bleating,
tube attached from mass to mass,

the slick itself turning vivid.
Whether there or in this floor-through,
Mother, I have missed you terribly—
miss you, though I know about
mothering myself.

*

This afternoon Madeline Carmichael, 61, was convicted
of fatally beating two-year-old Latanisha,

then embalming her body in newsprint, plastic,
and mothballs in a trunk in a closet

to keep her closest. The stench rose from that secret

threshold, made her presence alive for two decades

until Andres, ready to search for his twin,
asked his older sister Sabrina

what became of Latanisha

and the secret became memory
for the adult children. Until the cold case squad

attended to the painted-over closet,
though the mother told the super to evict

the ghost weeping in the vestibule

the remains had remained just that.

In the end that missing daughter
had come of age, moved out, was on her own

in the mother's infested imagination.

*

What search warrants uncover in a woman's closet
every one of us fears—and questions how one is capable

of fastening two small boys into blue car seats

and releasing the emergency brake to urge the Mazda
into the lake? to watch the car submerge

till nothing is left but disturbed surface scum?

*

So to that two-year-old on her mother's lap
in the little convertible in 1957
kicking and kicking her hard red Mary Janes
into her mother's knees even after
scolded—to *that her* inside me yet,

I will shush you all right. Make you
sit still. Make you nap the rest of the trip.
Imagine naming one *Latanisha*
and with the same hand that fed
bludgeoning her unconscious.

*

Scalding in a bathtub for soiling herself.

Locking in a trunk during a job interview.

Chaining to a radiator for breaking curfew.

Shaking for crying. Throwing out the window
for crying. Smothering with pillows for crying.

Stabbing for—something. Hitting for—

something else. Poisoning with paint thinner.
Imagine not feeding that bundle for days on end

because nothing can be done

but reside with the stench that is cell and self?

Goldsboro Narrative #45

The whites and the blacks are still newcomers.
You can tell: the way we claim flags, that we fight.
The other nomads were moved on, learning that land
does not love humans and is not at home with us,
even when it lets us grow ourselves food,
even when it lets us house our dead.
In some hundreds of years, this land will shrug us off
its wet and itching skin, tell us once more,
Get on.

Going to Hear My Child's Heartbeat
for the First Time—Part 2

it's the girl
in deep water
who will not drown

(drum)

come down

(drum)

come down

(drum)

zora's instrument
hidden in the belly

(drum)

carried
across the atlantic

(drum)

it's a mystery to master

(drum)

it don't stop

(drum)

don't stop

(drum)

gotta story to tell

      (drum)

won't stop

(drum)

gold-black fish

      (drum)

swimming

(drum)

an old one
come back

      (drum)

blood

(drum)

      breath

(drum)

      memory

(drum)

ka-doom   (drum)

ka-doom

(drum)

ka-doom   (drum)

live   (drum)

live   (drum)

live

Grass

San Antonio, Florida

They don't mow on Sundays in San Antonio.
They keep the seventh day for Paz
and Neruda, for Simic angels
whose wings are made of smoke.

And they walk their dogs softly in
the morning, so they will not miss
the smallest utterance of Whitman
or of John Clare, who pace the parks

early, when the ground fog's rising
and the oranges are lanterns
on their stems. And sometimes
they go to bed changed. And

they'll swear it was not they who
fumbled in their sheets at dawn,
as the poets rose like grass, and
the mowers coughed and were still.

Gospel of the Two Sisters

Long ago two sisters lived in a small brick house beside a super-highway. The tall chatty one knew the first & last name of every animal in the galaxy. The small quiet one could make her hair grow longer or shorter with no more than a thought.

The pecan-colored sister said, "I wish I had the shiny exoskeleton of the *Monomorium minimum*," & when the penny-colored sister squinted her eyes, hair spilled across the floors & they had carpet.

But the girls had no other relatives or friends & eventually they grew sick of each other. One day the sister with the gold hoop earrings said the mastiff, a large, powerful, short-haired dog, is ancestor of the pit bull, the boxer, & the Saint Bernard, but it is the ugliest breed of them all & then, after a few unusual moments of silence, said: "Sister, do you ever wished we had a mother or father to braid our hair?"

The sister with the banana-colored press-on nails rolled her eyes & though she was stone-faced, her hair began to weep & she looked suddenly like someone who'd been walking in the rain.

I can remember how I came to believe in God. I was sitting one Sunday in the front row listening to three dirt-old deacons sing an a cappella "Amazing Grace" when a trembling like fingers through a tub of warm water passed through me. I opened my mouth & there was a feeling like the time my cousin Junebug put me in the Sleeper Hold until I blacked out.

For many years afterward the sister that could sprint eighty miles without stopping paced up & down the hallway waiting for the right sentence to worm into her ear or push out of her mouth & the sister that could sleep underwater sat in a rocking chair await-ing the same thing.

Then the sisters discovered they were pregnant & each gave birth to a boy on the same dry September day. The sister with the tattoo of Joe Frazier bought every bit of baby blue in the city & countryside for her son & dressed him in a new outfit every sixty minutes. The sister with eyes like two bowls of black bean soup bought every children's book ever written, & began reading them nonstop as soon as her son grew ears.

The sons said they just wanted to be sung to.

How often do you hear the tenderness you need to hear? I mean exactly when you need to hear it? Is it ever before that little yolk of hurt wraps itself in layers of contempt hard enough to break teeth?

The sister with the overbite asked the sister with bullet in her hip, "Do we even remember how to sing?" They had not spoken to each other in several years so they'd forgotten the sound words made fluttering between them. Then the son with the buckethead smiled at the son with elephant ears & the sisters' scratchy, awkward gospel began to unravel & drift across the room.

A Postcard from Okemah

Turned from the camera's eye, hovering,
between river & bridge, the hung woman
looks downstream, & snagged in the air
beside her, the body of her young son.

They are tassels on a drawn curtain;
they are the closed eyes of the black boy
who will find them while leading his cow
to the riverbank; they are the bells

that will clang around the animal's neck
when it lowers its head to drink.
Mother & son caught in *Without Sanctuary,*
a book of American lynchings.

The boy dangles in midair
like a hooked fish, his pants hanging
from his ankles like a tail fin.
On the bridge women pose

in aprons & feathered bonnets,
the men wear wide-brimmed hats
with bowties or dungarees;
there are three small girls leaning

against the railing & a boy nestled
beneath the wing of his father's arm.
I count sixty-seven citizens & children
staring at what must have been a flash

& huff of smoke. The photographer
must have stood on a boat deck,
though from this angle
he could have been standing on the water

with his arms outstretched.
He must have asked them to smile
at the camera & later, scrawled his copyright
& condolences on the back of the postcards

he made for the murdered man's friends.
"The Negroes got what would have been due
to them under process of the law,"
the sheriff said. Words necessary

for everyone to sleep. His deputy
had been shot when the posse searched
the suspects' cabin for stolen meat.
To protect her son, the woman claimed

she'd fired the gun. Her innocence,
the papers said, was determined weeks
before the mob dragged them both
from the jail bound by saddle string.

If you look closely you can see a pattern
of tiny flowers printed upon her dress;
you can see an onlooker's hand opened
as if he's just released a dark bouquet.

Now all of Okemah, Oklahoma,
with its barrooms & pep rallies,
its stalled tractors & wedding showers,
with its beauty parlors & barbecues, is hushed.

Now even the children in attendance are dead.
After that day in 1911, it did not rain again.
Newborns died suckling breasts filled with dust.
To believe in God, this is the reckoning I claim.

It is a Monday morning ninety years too late.
All the rocking chairs & shopping carts,
all the mailboxes & choir pews are empty.
I cannot hear the psalms of salvation

or forgiveness, the gospel of Mercy.
I cannot ask who is left more disfigured:
the ones who are beaten or the ones who beat;
the ones who are hung or the ones who hang.

Aretha at Fame Studios

I could speak on a hotter than fire riot
time and a woman tying up her Detroit
promises in a rag. The prodigal child
arriving in Muscle Shoals, Alabama—hopefully
to sing freedom if only for one day.
The migration head swallowing its tail in the year of my birth.
I'm telling the truth when I say she'll meet Dr. King soon.
He'll kiss her on the cheek, tell her (damn
straight) she should demand what's due her.
And you could eat a tune served up more
than a few times, ripe pot liquor
settled around the old meat of the matter.
And I could forget the deal; she's here for business,
not to march. See the white musicians in the studio with her,
not a brother's guitar anywhere in sight?
Young boys playing so good like they've been chased
through the swamps for decades. Like they know
talk going on underneath a sister's clothes.
They got the nerve to have their eyes wide open.
She lifts her voice, starts telling tales out of school,
You're a no-good heartbreaker
and is there any doubt about the color
of the man she conjures? I could discuss her signature
key now but I'm afraid she has raised him
from the dust, he's standing on the other
side of glass and that next note, that next note
might cause him to break fool in front of white folks.
You're a no-good heartbreaker
Somebody stop that man.
Somebody stop that man.
Somebody stop that sister from hollering

the naming his sins out loud blues.
Somebody close these white folks' eyes.
Somebody lie to her and keep her from crying.
Somebody tell her a little bit of sweetness
is coming her way quick.

out

on daddy's farm, the stallions we snared and stormed into dirt would rear high to stuff their mouths with sun, buck to kick stars out of sky. rope and spur seared servitude's lesson through muscle and bone till they broke beneath brand. sometimes, i would stoop far and slow in front of them, low enough to squint up into fence crazed eyes and make it plain: i would smolder there till beast learned to labor with man on its back or till we whispered for the twelve gauge shout of slavery's leaden psalm through its brain.

orphaned, swollen with texas roadside dust, i sit here counting broken years between youth's lapping tongue and the cellblock's crushing fifteen year kiss. i am a cinder on the prairie, bruise on the horizon purpling sundown's sky. i push prison's gunmetal bit from between teeth, spit sun from my head to see straight, wipe hope's stardust from heel before loading each shackle scar into my gunnysack of voice. this is how i cipher my way home, stumble my way back to a shreveport woman's arms.

freedom

freedom is what you can buy with a song. after the song has been soldered into your lungs. after the song has beaten its way inside your dreams. after the song has snuck its way into your bed. after the song has knuckled you under. after the song has festered and blossomed and festered again. after the song has stolen your fingers and robbed your voice blind. after all this, you try to sell the song that can never be sold. you end up with your hand out, waiting for the words that spell freedom.

freedom is every dirt road ground into whiskey still of my voice, my backpocket buck knife blade sharpening silence, coiled up close to copperhead, dime and dollar bill, the price of a pint and the slow violence of a victrola spittin' bessie's blues. freedom is my baby's tit in my palm, a song in the sweetback sling of her legs, the snakeoil slide of dreadnaught guitar string strung and standing hard in darkened dayroom corners. freedom lurches in and out of my life heavy as the swollen secret of a noose.

April

one robin, one yellow willow
love braving the rain on the wrong highway—
honestly, I don't know what to think!

a Canada goose, a headlong cloud

Open the window!
under my hand, your wet skin
you looking?

thirty April mornings

one white tulip, one red

one precise interior
one persistent stem

2

cherry blossom, silver bridge

don't ever take my sweet
for weak

peaches! peaches! April
has no way to get there yet

quiet room, roaring sky

April, I'm almost over you
    again

Trash Traders

That's how it starts, with the trash. Someone is swapping the trash, silently and insidiously, all over town. On the Promenade des Aubes, the rich lift the lids of their silvery pails and find used Pampers stuffed into empty boxes of Hamburger Helper; well-bred aunts hold up low-watt bulbs and shake them gingerly, as if the gritty rattle could give them a clue to how these dim, gray globes got there. At first they are perplexed; some feel menaced, but everyone is too embarrassed to ask questions. How can we take our friends aside, they ask, our neighbors, and accuse them of nosing about in our trash? We are a private and well-behaved community, with good personal habits.

The poor, meanwhile, find the rich people's salads. As they huddle in their meager dwellings along Petroleum Parkway, they cannot comprehend the meaning of the lacy red lettuce leaves that flutter faintly in their stinking, dented cans, nor the strange, fibrous spices like the branches of febrile underwater plants. In the lanes, nameless and grim, their children finger the thick cast-off stationery of the affluent—ivory laid, embossed, and stenciled, with words like "the Hon." and "Esq."—and wonder what has happened to their grease-spotted newsprint which balled so easily, so satisfyingly, in the fist.

Class distinctions grow fuzzy, causing car collisions, as no one knows whom to stop for in traffic. That is bad enough, but the mess soon becomes professional—the Banking District smeared with coal mine soot, the Garment District mysteriously studded with spittoons. Shirtwaist sweatshops pump out rolled cigars, bagels, and film. Where can you go for a proper haircut, a hot dog, or an airtight will? Nobody knows.

It's the next phase that's personal. Intimate. Male garbage surfacing, shockingly, in female receptacles. And vice versa. Inevitably, gender distinctions blur, for how can a man pronounce himself a bachelor when he finds his Rubbermaid loaded with sodden Maxipads? What's worse is the decadence, the trash of debauchery staining the sacks of the innocent. Condoms in kiddie garbage, the lids stamped with grimacing Ronald McDonald, his hair an alarming carrot, his tongue lolling, blue, diseased. Spinsters, disposing of frayed thread and yogurt cups, are assaulted by the garbage of a family of five—used coloring books, bicycle grease, congealed macaroni flowing out in a great vomitus from their demure wicker baskets.

Predictably, people suffer identity crises. For who are we, if not what we leave behind? To know our refuse is to know ourselves, what we have used and consumed, fondled, rejected, outgrown. But what have we thrown away? All of a sudden, we recognize in our trash bins the very items we cannot do without—riches in our shredders, silky and spangled, mysteries in our dumpsters, looming and lush. These are hints to hidden identities, these are found objets d'art—behold the sculpture of gum in an ashtray, the ambiance of a tattered lampshade. "How could I have thrown that away?" housewives gasp, clutching discarded lint and empty cans of lard as if they are lost children. Soon everyone is saving lemon rinds, dried snot, and flat tires; they cling to boll weevils, Spam, and shopping mall tunes. Those of a more cerebral bent memorize ISBN numbers, thread counts, and the etymology of the word "aardvark." Meanwhile, people are throwing away their beds, their doors, their meat, not to mention first kisses and favorite scatological jokes.

And yet, who is to say? What, after all, is trash, is *refuse*—what is fit to be flicked, chucked, flung? How does anyone know what to throw away and what to keep safe, secure, and orderly, in their homes and in their minds? Why don't they commit to memory the words of a television jingle for baked beans, let's say, or for flexible flea collars, and forget the ages of their children, the taste of grandmother's tomato sauce, or their own favorite color?

As priorities shift throughout the city, people find themselves forgetting. Yes, they can rattle off the capitals of tiny island nations, but how abashedly they stammer when it comes to Beethoven (was that the Minister of Culture under Hitler? or a German cooking utensil?). They know the Latin term for blowfish but grope for the names of their wives, friends, mothers-in-law. Soon they've forgotten their own and fall into addressing each other as Joe, Bob, and Merle. They grow confused on their way home, brokers banging on doors of tract homes, demanding Scotch and soda of hapless Peruvian women they imagine they wed in a ballroom some June day long ago. They get lost on their way to work; window dressers climb into buses and drive them into billboards, piano tuners traipse into hospitals and put on scrubs. Many die or lose their spleens. The great maestros of the keyboard wither with shame when they bang their concertos out of key, causing mass exoduses from packed concert halls. Tuxedo tails flap madly like bats from a cave.

Panic ensues. The streets teem with people, rushing and jouncing each other, stumbling on loose trash. "Where are we going?" some of them cry, but more are asking, "Where did we come from?," a much more frightening question. No one can remember which memories they cast away and which they merely appropriated, like borrowed umbrellas in an unexpected downpour. "My mother was a war nurse," boldly states one wizened old man, then, with a buckling of the knees, "or was that yours?" "I was a war nurse!" a woman cries out, but she is already being swept away by the current of the crowd. "I am your mother!" She is no more than eighteen.

Quiet finally settles on the streets. Everyone has been swept up in piles like so many leaves, so dried up, exhausted, that they fall into oblivion, welcome it with the relief of resignation. Eyes stop darting, and limbs stop twitching, and everyone listens only to the wind, the empty air stirring and spinning the newspapers and dead flowers and Styrofoam cups that lie piled in the gutters so thickly, so softly. It seems that the wind makes a whispering sound, almost murmurs a song, almost forms words they almost think they recognize, while all around them their earthly possessions, weightless and threadbare, lift and blow away. In fact, they barely notice as everything they've discarded rises up in a gentle, growing whirl, gusting and circling around its axis of dirt and dreams and small gleaming details stored up and tossed away too randomly, too carelessly, even to be mourned.

Iowa Winter

The week Junior died, the temperature dropped to fourteen below and stayed there. The seats on my Honda felt like they were made of plywood, and the engine groaned before turning over, a low sound like some Japanese movie monster waking up after a thousand-year sleep. I had long underwear on under my suit, but I could still feel my legs numbing up. Four miles to the funeral parlor, and the heater never did kick in.

After it was over, we all went back to Louise's for food. There was a big ham her sister, June, had brought down from Madison, and the girls, Maddy and Chris, were there with their husbands and kids. Louise had made chicken and seven-layer salad and brownies, and there was plenty to drink, too. I went to work on some wine and also took responsibility for the music. I played Willie Nelson's *Stardust* album, because I remembered Junior had liked it, and because I did, too.

Louise got me alone about an hour into it and pointed out toward the porch, where a lone person stood all bundled up smoking a cigarette. "What am I supposed to do now?" she said.

"We all knew this was coming. It has to be a bit of a relief." I didn't quite know what she was driving at.

"Not about Junior—that is a relief." She pointed again. "I mean about him. About Clay."

I sipped some more wine. It was good stuff—better than I'd buy for myself. I get the Mediterranean red, which is cheap but drinkable. "A man who'll step outside for a cigarette in this weather has to really love to smoke," I said. "I might join him."

"I don't think he has any plans," she said. "Neither of them did. And now that Junior is gone, I'm afraid he's just going to stay."

All along, I'd done my best not to think too hard about Clay and Junior. They'd met at a support group—I knew that. Coffee, cookies, a musty room in the basement of some school. The spring before, with Junior's health deteriorating fast, he'd moved back into the house, and Clay had come along. They looked the same—

skinny and getting skinnier, big, hollowed-out eyes. Going through the same hell, it was easier to have each other there. I don't believe they were being boyfriends together, exactly—they were both too weak. Mostly, they watched TV, drank sodas, and smoked cigarettes, counted out each other's pills. It was a good thing that Clay was around, particularly these last months, since it took some of the burden off Louise. But now I could see the problem.

"Can't he go home to his people?"

"His people don't want him. They disowned him a long time ago."

"Maybe he should have thought about that when he decided to embrace an alternate lifestyle."

"I can't go through it all again. You don't know how bad it was. With your own son, that's one thing. A person can do it. But I'm really afraid. You know how you read about old people, and when their spouse dies, they just suddenly lose their own desire to live?" She looked at me. Our problems were different. I had drunk myself out of this marriage ten years ago, but it didn't mean we weren't in love.

"You think he's going to die now?"

"I don't think it, I know it. And I won't have it happen here. There's only so much a person can do."

"What do you want from me?" I said.

"Tell him he has to leave."

I looked out at the figure on the porch. It was cold enough to freeze birds right out of the air, and he was calmly finishing his cigarette. A person in the process of moving right beyond his body. "Me?"

"Please, Lenny?" she said.

The twins, Kayla and Kaylin, ran past us giggling, each of them clutching ham sandwiches. "Those girls sure can eat," I said. "Maddy might want to think about putting them on a diet."

I used to have a nice little house-painting business. After I sold that, I drove truck for R. C. Reynolds up in Cedar Rapids, mostly routes in the Midwest. Paper products. Then I started to get back trouble, L-4 and L-5 to be exact, and at fifty I went on disability. I was already out of the house, set up in my own place out here by the river. It flooded the first year, bad, and you can still see the marks on walls where the water came to. I drank beer at the time, and I remember how when I came back from a week on Louise's sofa to survey the damage, my empties were floating around in the middle of the living room like barrel-shaped aluminum fish. Insurance eventually took care of most of it, but I learned fast that life by myself wasn't necessarily going to be a big bachelor party.

My second day in the house, before the flood, Louise came by with a bunch of dinners in Tupperware, each labeled neatly across the top: "Lasagna," "Meatloaf," "Soup Beans," and "Chinese." I didn't know what she meant by that last one, and I never did open it to see what was inside. It's still there. When I want Chinese, I'll usually go into town and head to Ding's for the lunch special.

For a couple of days after the funeral, I thought about it. I didn't want to get involved, particularly, but I did want to be helpful. This Clay person and I had at least one thing in common, which was that we'd been disowned by the people that loved us because of our behavior. In my case it was drinking and causing scenes, in his it was having sex with men. We didn't have to do these things. I knew that Junior's getting sick was more or less inevitable. Before he ever turned up back in Iowa City from San Francisco, I figured there was something wrong. He was still healthy then, still shiny and optimistic, talking about how he was going to write children's books, signing up for classes at the University. But I understood why he was back, and Louise did, too. And when he started to lose weight and get sick, we didn't ever even say the word, but we all knew. He was taking almost forty pills a day by the end.

I went by to see Clay. It was a weekday, and Louise was at work up at the hospital. I had a drink first, of course—Early Times on the rocks. It was good, but it didn't prepare me for what it felt like to step outside. Even with the sun shining, the air was like a smack in the face. The river was solid as concrete, and the spidery limbs of the naked trees made me think of cracks in a windshield. I wondered if weather like this made them shut down completely, or if underneath it all they were still growing.

Clay was watching television in the living room. "Hey," he said, when I came in.

"Hey yourself." I stood over him. His cigarettes were on the coffee table, along with a can of Pepsi and a partially completed crossword puzzle. He was in jeans and a short-sleeved shirt that was too big for him, and that it occurred to me might have been one of my old ones. "You want to get out of here for a while? Go get one of them three-dollar coffees?"

He grinned, showing teeth as yellow as a horse's. He needed a shave, too. "All right," he said. "You buying?"

"I am."

We didn't talk in the car. I found a space right out front to the Coffee Company, fed the meter a couple of quarters, and we went in. He got a cappuccino, and I had a Siddartha, which the sign translated as "breakfast blend."

"That's a novel by Hesse," Clay said.

"I know it." We headed away from the counter up front and back into an unoccupied sofa that looked like it had come straight from some old lady's attic without any vacuuming in between. He sat on that, and I settled onto a chair opposite. There was a little table in between us. "It's still a dumb name for a cup of coffee." Someone walked past us with a teapot on a tray. "You know what 'chai' is?" I said. "It's Japanese for 'tea.' You order 'chai tea,' that's like asking for a 'sandwich sandwich.'"

We sipped our drinks. The place was relatively quiet—a couple of tables away a grad-student type was clicking away at his laptop. A middle-aged woman was reading a book. Light jazz drifted down from hidden speakers somewhere above us.

"I think I can guess what this is about," Clay said, finally.

"What?"

"Well, when Louise had that trouble with the dishwasher, she called you to come look at it. And you fixed it the next day."

"Yeah."

"And you fixed that step out front last fall."

"I can do a couple of things."

"You want me to go."

"It's not me that wants it, exactly."

"Right. I get it."

I was thinking how easy this was. He understood the situation. I took another sip of coffee and felt something nice and comfortable kick in, like it does after the first drink of the evening. "So then it's understood? What needs to happen?"

Clay leaned forward. I could see all the bones in his face. "Lenny," he said. "There is no place."

"Sure there is. Don't you have a friend you could stay with?"

His eyes held on to mine. "Junior was my friend. Junior was everything."

"I appreciate that. But Junior is gone. You knew this was going to happen—both of you did. Didn't you ever talk about it? Didn't you ever plan?"

"No," he said. "We didn't plan."

"Well, that wasn't that smart, then, was it?"

"Maybe not."

"You can't expect my wife to take care of you."

"I won't bother anyone. She won't even notice I'm there."

"What are you going to do?"

"I don't know," he said. "It's something I've been thinking about. There was really just one thing I did up until last week, and that was take care of Junior. Without him, I'm kind of at a loss." He laughed nervously. He had a very deep voice, croaky from all the smoking he did.

"What about your folks?"

"They don't know where I am, and they never will."

"I'm sorry," I said. "It sounds like a tough situation. I'm just here to tell you that you need to find alternate accommodations. Let's say in a week, all right? Louise—my wife—this past year has been hard on her, as you can imagine."

"You think this hasn't been hard on me?" For a second, I saw something rise up in him, a tough-sonofabitch independence that turned on a yellow light in his dead eyes, then went away. I recognized it, and I respected it. He took another swallow of his drink, and some froth clung to the corner of his mouth.

"I tell you what," I said. "You can come camp with me, temporarily. The important thing is that we get you out of Louise's hair. It's not a permanent solution, but I can live with it for a little while." After I'd said it, I was a little sorry. But it was out there, and I wasn't going to take it back.

"I don't think so." He stared down at the table.

"Where will you go, then?"

He didn't answer. His face looked all clammy.

"You okay?"

"Coffee is hard on my stomach."

"Then you shouldn't drink it."

"I like to drink it."

"I'm giving you an out here," I said. "Be careful, because I don't have to do it. But I know that you meant something to Junior, and that carries weight."

"All right," he said, so quietly, I could barely hear.

I dropped Clay back at Louise's and told him he could move in the next day. Then I went to the library and did some reading. After that I headed over to the Deadwood and drank a couple more Early Times and started chatting up Nicole, the bartender. She's got enormous patience when it comes to me. One time she even drove me home, and it's not remotely on her way. I was so drunk, apparently, I started reciting Shakespeare, and I don't know any. She put me to bed and everything.

"Cold enough for you?" I said.

"Come on, Lenny," she said. "I don't get paid enough to listen to 'cold enough for you.'"

"You ever know anyone with AIDS?"

"Yeah." She lit up a cigarette and offered me one, which I took. She's got pretty hair. Graduated a few years ago with a degree in art, still trying to figure out what to do with it. "Why?"

"I'm taking in a roommate. Friend of my son's."

"I'm so sorry. I heard about him."

"It's okay. Life wasn't treating him so good. Now we got this other guy on our hands, see. You think it might be dangerous?"

"Not if you practice safe sex."

"That's not even funny. I mean silverware and stuff. Dishes. Just breathing the same air. Stuff hangs. I saw this program once where they showed what a sneeze does. Droplets in the air. You ever heard of 'HAART'?"

"'Heart' like valentines? Like the kind that are always getting broken?"

"It stands for 'Highly Active Anti-Retroviral Therapy.'"

"I know some of those words."

"Otherwise known as the cocktail approach."

"You mean pills."

I nodded and pointed to my glass, which was empty. I could

feel a pretty good glow getting started, too, and I had an idea. The Early Times bottle behind the bar was about half full. I decided I would spend the afternoon killing it off and that would be it—after that I was through with drinking. I'd always known that someday I'd quit, and today seemed as good as any other. "I know a little something about the cocktail approach myself," I said.

Nicole smiled prettily. She had on big hoop earrings and a black turtleneck that showed off those small, high breasts of hers. "What do you know about it?"

"I know that it only works for so long."

I spent the whole afternoon at the Deadwood. Around dinner time, I drunk-drove over to the house, passing by the time and temperature sign outside the First National Bank which announced minus-15 in numbers lit yellow against the dark sky. As I parked, I was conscious of all the normal lives around me in those 1920's-era houses, and I leaned on my horn just to wake them up a little. Ours was on Bank Street, a nice screened porch out front that I'd done quite a bit of work on over the years—jacked it up where it sagged, painted it, put in new steps. Louise's car was in the driveway—we drive the same model, though hers is a few years newer—so I knew she was home. I also knew she wouldn't want to see me like this, but that never stopped me before.

She was in the kitchen, but she came out to the living room when she heard me come in. She'd changed out of her work clothes into jeans and a big green T-shirt, and she had a knife in her hand. "Was that you honking?" she said.

"Hell, no. Louis Armstrong is out there. He's thinking to himself, 'What a wonderful world.'"

"You are sauced. Go on home. And try not to kill anyone on the way."

"I'm celebrating."

"What?" She gave me a puzzled look. "What are you celebrating? Did the price of whiskey go down?" She moved past me and gave the door a shove, since I hadn't closed it all the way. "I don't even want to think about the next heating bill."

"Where is he?" I said.

"Upstairs, resting."

"I quit drinking this afternoon."

"Go look in the bathroom mirror, then come back and say that again."

I needed to go anyway, so I plowed through the kitchen and into the little powder room we have off it. The temperature in there was a good twenty degrees colder than the rest of the house, but the plumbing wasn't froze up yet, and the toilet flushed just fine. The man in the mirror looked pretty good for his age. Still had all his hair, only some of it gray. Could have used a shave and a haircut. I picked a fleck of something out from between my upper teeth and tried to remember the last thing I'd had to eat. It looked vegetable, but I didn't think I'd had any.

When I came back out, she was chopping mushrooms.

"What's for dinner?"

"You can take home the rest of that ham Maddy brought. It's in the fridge. And the seven-layer salad—there's plenty, and it needs to be eaten soon. Did you do anything at all about what I asked?"

"Asked?"

"Oh, Lenny."

I picked a mushroom off the table and popped it whole into my mouth. "Of course. He'll be out of here tomorrow."

"He will? Where is he going?"

"Never mind about that. We've discussed it. I got him out of your hair. Call me for the tough jobs." The mushroom was dry in my mouth, and I stuck my head under the faucet to get some water to wash it down with.

She put down the knife. I saw that she was crying, just a little. "Thank you," she said, in a tiny voice that just about broke me down, too. "You don't know."

"At least things will be easier for you around here."

"It's like some strange shadow he left behind. With the wasting, they even look the same."

"It's okay," I said, "I've got everything under control." I reached out for another mushroom and knocked the entire cutting board to the floor.

I slept until noon the next day. Then I called to see if Clay was ready, and he was, so I drove over to pick him up. He was dressed in jeans he had to keep hitching up, and a dark green University of Iowa sweatshirt. He had two duffel bags full of clothes and an oversized leather briefcase. "Going to the office?" I asked.

"Meds," he said.

I stopped at Hy-Vee first so we could get some food, as I didn't have anything around the house. "What do you like?" I said. "How about we cook up some chili? Put some meat on those bones of yours."

We bought hamburger, chili mix, beans, canned tomatoes, Minute Rice, a 12-pack of Pepsi, Pop-Tarts, chocolate chip cookies, Steak-Umms, some frozen burritos, and a dozen bananas, among other things. When we passed by the beer aisle, I first looked the other way, then picked out a six of O'Doul's. My head felt like donkeys had trampled it during the night, but the feeling wasn't an unfamiliar one, and in a way, I sort of savored it, since I didn't figure to ever feel that way again. As we were headed for the checkout line, it seemed to me Clay was getting antsy.

"They got a bathroom in this place?" he whispered.

"Probably. You gotta go?"

"Uh-huh. Bad."

"Can't it wait?"

"I don't think so."

I flagged down a kid who was on his way to shelve some bread. He pointed back toward Frozen Foods, and Clay hurried off. I paid for the groceries and stood by the entrance reading the little notices posted there on the bulletin board. Tractor for sale. AKC-registered Collie pups. A trailer for rent in Tipton. Hockey skates, barely used, $20. I thought about how Junior and I used to skate together sometimes, and then I tried to remember where our skates might be, or if they'd gotten thrown away somewhere along the line. Finally, Clay showed up. His face didn't have much color to begin with, but now, under those store lights, he looked positively bleached.

"You all right?" I asked.

"I don't really want to talk about it."

"Jesus Christ," I said. "All right, let's go."

Clay cleaned himself up, and we had dinner, which I thought came out pretty good. We ate the way I always ate, in front of the television. Afterwards, I dug around the basement and found the skates. I brought them up and asked him what size his feet were. He was in the middle of taking two blue pills. That briefcase of his was divided up into sections, color-coded. Some of the pills had to be taken before meals, some with them, and some after. Others were for first thing in the morning or last thing before bed.

"Ten," he said.

"Bingo." I held out the box. "Try these on."

Something like a smile flickered over his face and went away. In general, for expressions, he reminded me of those scrambled cable channels I sometimes found myself watching late at night—most of the time there's nothing there, but every now and then, like magic, the picture would come in clear as day. "Junior told me he used to play hockey. I got weak ankles."

"What's the difference?" I said. "I got a bad back. We could still lace 'em up and give it a shot for fifteen minutes or so. That river out there, it's like glass."

"You're nuts," he said. "Look at me."

"Come on. Believe in yourself." I held out the box, and he took it.

Just the effort of lacing them up wore him out—I could see it. He was breathing hard and sweating, and leaning forward he farted, which I made a point of laughing at to make him feel okay. I was sorry. Those ankles were like something you see on the History Channel, like something the Nazis did. His feet might have been tens, but he still swum in the skates, and it just made me think of Junior, and how I'd used to take him up to the field house Sundays to play with the Rec league, what a solid young man he'd been. I started thinking hard about whether I had anything to drink in the house.

"I'm not much of an athlete," said Clay, attempting to stand. "I play a pretty good game of backgammon, though, if you've got it." He teetered for a moment, then fell back onto the sofa. "We going?"

"It's too cold," I said. "I don't know what I was thinking. But maybe if this breaks over the next day or two, and you're still here, we could."

I set him up in the guest bedroom, and he was asleep by ten. I could hear him snoring back there, surrounded by boxes full of my junk, old magazines and fishing tackle, a TV I'd been trying to repair on and off for years, a dusty 1985 IBM-clone computer (no hard drive) and amber monitor that never did work right in the first place, but that I'd hung on to because I don't know why. I wondered what the hell I'd gotten myself into. I was feeling irritable, so I brushed my teeth, and when I was done I swished Listerine around in my mouth, but instead of spitting, I swallowed. That tasted truly awful, but it also gave me a sudden view of myself as no better than those kids you read about huffing paint, so I made myself a pot of coffee and drank half of it while watching a lunatic Australian on television prance around the desert picking up snakes. And all the while, I could feel the cold outside pushing in at the walls. Nature is hostile, no matter how hard we try to convince ourselves the opposite.

The next day I was sick. I hadn't gone twenty-four hours without a drink in years, and my body was in rebellion. Or maybe it was the flu. My stomach was loose, and I was running a low fever. Clay planted himself in my living room and did pretty much what he'd been doing back at the house, which was watch daytime TV and smoke, only here he didn't have to go outside. He did a fair amount of coughing, too. For a while, I came out and joined him, and we sat and stared at the shows together—he liked the crime ones, when they were on, but he also didn't mind the talk ones—but then I started to feel shaky again, and I went back to bed. About an hour later I woke up, and he was sitting on the edge of my bed, staring down at me.

"What's your problem?" I said.

"I was just wondering if there's anything I could do for you."

"Do? I don't know. Can you mix a good martini?"

He laughed. "Probably. It's been a while. Junior used to tell me about a place he went to in San Francisco—the Zam Zam Room. Some strange old codger bartended, and he made the best martinis on the planet, but you had to be really careful. Like, if you looked at him the wrong way, he'd throw you out. So you put your money on the bar and just waited to be spoken to. After he made you your drink, he'd tell you where you were allowed to sit. If you just went to a table and sat without him telling you, that was it—you wouldn't get served."

"You weren't out in San Francisco?" I asked.

"Me? No. I grew up in Moline. I never been west of Sioux City.

Been to New York a couple of times. I liked that." I saw that face of his flicker again, this time with memories I was pretty sure I wanted no part of.

"Okay, listen," I said. "It's nice of you to ask, but don't come in here again without knocking, all right?"

He stood. "That was a joke, then, about the martini?"

There were ants crawling around inside my eyeballs; I felt all jittery. "I'm reforming my life," I told him. "This here what I'm going through, it's the necessary pain."

For dinner, we had leftover chili. I washed mine down with two cans of O'Doul's, and Clay had his usual Pepsi. We weren't talking, we were just eating. Then right in the middle of taking a bite, he put his fork back into his bowl and started to cry. I wasn't sure where to look. I had another bite, but what appetite I'd managed to convince myself I had was gone. There were visible cobwebs in a corner of the ceiling, and I reminded myself to remember them next time I vacuumed.

"Sorry," he said, when he'd more or less pulled himself back together.

"Yeah, well. Sometimes it can all get to be a lot."

"I wish I could skate." He was on verge of losing it again. "I wish a ton of things. I never even got to be in a real love affair. Me and Junior, it was just a couple of young guys in old men's bodies."

"Hey, hey. This is his father you're talking to. I don't need to hear that."

He sniffed, blew his nose into one of the paper towels we were using as napkins. "Why don't you live at the house with Louise?"

"She asked me to leave. I wasn't very reliable. Used to disappear sometimes for a couple of days at a time. I might have hit her once or twice. But people can change. You know what you need? A project."

"I know it."

"I'm serious. You can't sit around watching TV all the time—you'll turn into a blob. What can you do?"

"Nothing," he said. "Last six months, it was all about Junior. Giving him sponge baths, cleaning up his messes, helping him in and out of bed, just everything."

I'd been in denial about this. When I had stopped over, which wasn't often, they usually had him already out on the sofa, cleaned up and ready to receive visitors. I hadn't wanted to know what went on behind the scenes. "You think that's where you're headed?"

He stirred his chili and didn't answer.

Then I got another idea. I was full of them these days. "What about that book he was working on? Do you know anything about that? Maybe you could finish it up. I know this girl in town, she's an artist. I could put you two together. She's a very good friend. What was it called?"

"*A City Dog.* Louise has it."

"That's great. Kids love dog stories. My grandkids do—all of them. Nothing better than a dog story. What do you say?"

"You don't understand. I have no talent. Junior was a good writer. He was musical, too. Some people just aren't born with that."

This was news to me. I tried to think of one musical thing I could remember Junior doing. I tried to think of one thing I could remember him writing. I could vaguely remember some finger paintings on the refrigerator door, but I suspected these were Kayla and Kaylin's, and it worried me that last week and thirty years ago weren't more clearly separated in my mind.

"Well, you think about it. I'll write down this girl's number for you, and maybe you'll give her a call. Might be a nice tribute to Junior, and maybe you could sell it and make a little money. I'm guessing you don't have any, right?"

I could see sweat coming out on his face, and I was conscious of it on my own, too. "I got some in the bank. Not much. I get disability."

"Me, too," I said. "God bless the government. Will you think about it?"

"Yes, sir," he said.

"That's all I want to hear."

He went to bed early again, and again I stayed up. This time I watched *The African Queen,* but seeing Bogart toss back whole mugs of gin made me change over to a biography of Rock Hudson, which was only slightly less depressing. Louise used to tell me I looked like him, back when we were dating, after I got out of the Army, and it made me feel funny now, thinking back, because who would have ever pegged him for gay? And yet there it was, right on the TV, about how he was going out to sex places and bath houses, and all the while pretending that he was married to that sexy Susan St. James. Louise hadn't known the first thing about Rock Hudson, and I hadn't known the first thing about my own son, and I wondered if anyone really knew anything about anything, or if we were all just making it up, blind people walking through the world with our arms outstretched, guessing.

I slept hard, but not well. I dreamed burglars were coming—I even heard them open the sliding glass door to the living room. They took everything—the TV, my computer, the furniture, my great-grandpa's revolver from when he was security on the Union Pacific Railroad. They took all the silverware, even though it was just stuff I'd picked up at Target. They took all the framed family photos Louise had given me over the years. I knew they were doing this, but I stayed put in my bed, huddled, pretending to be asleep, not coming out until I was sure they'd left. When I did, I found they hadn't closed the door. Snow—it was snowing in my dream—drifted in and filled half the living room, sparkling and fine like sifted sugar, and I had to shovel it out.

I awoke conscious that it really *was* cold in the house, and I pulled on some sweats and slippers. In the living room, the door was open, although just a crack, and there was no snow. I pushed it shut, shivering, went to the thermostat, and cranked up the heat. Only then did it occur to me how quiet everything was. Just the sound of the furnace cranking on and warmed air breathing up out of the vents.

I didn't need to check his room. I put on jeans and boots and a parka and hat and gloves, got a flashlight, and walked down to the water's edge. There's a little worn path that leads there, and at the end of it I nearly stumbled over a pair of high-top sneakers. Playing the light out onto the ice, I saw a shape about forty yards upriver, where Clay appeared to be lying flat on his back.

I tested the ice with one foot before stepping onto it, even though it was frozen hard enough to support an eighteen-wheeler. Then I walked out to him. He'd put on the skates again, apparently outside, which seemed miraculous, given how cold it was.

Yet somehow he'd gotten them laced and tied. He was bare-chest-ed—his shirt and undershirt lay on the ice a few feet away, and his rib cage stood out prominently, descending fast to an almost non-existent stomach that ended where his too-large khakis began. I learned later that one of the final sensations a person freezing to death feels is intense heat. It's so uncomfortable that you are likely to tear off all your own clothes to try and get cool—this is one of the reasons that homeless people found dead of exposure are often assumed to also have been victims of sex crimes. But even without that knowledge, it didn't seem so odd to see Clay that way, arms and legs extended, almost like a person making a snow angel. His eyes were closed as if he were asleep, and an unlit ciga-rette jutted up casually from between his lips. The ice nearby was all marked up from where he'd wobbled around on those things, those skates of my son's.

I went inside to call Louise, late as it was.

Letter to Alice

I'm up in Squaw Valley—yes the name is utterly inappropriate
in these late twentieth-century days, but hey, history
isn't pretty especially place names.

Monument Valley has no monuments
The Eiffel Tower or *Tour Eiffel* just stands there
squat on the ground, then rises grid and girders.

The difference between New York and Paris is landmarks.
A tower for tourists. A bridge connecting boroughs
You can walk on both, but where does the tower take you?

But back to you. Your poetry is now in the hands of critics
far-flung. Like starlings they peck at loaves of text
—forgive that awful metaphor—

I know you must find this thrilling or pitiful depending on
the tenor of gray that manifests itself as Parisian sky
Light gray—mist, darker gray—rain, rain, rain.

Thinking about the Myth of Alice Notley
Everyone wants just that one touch of your Irish wit, if indeed
it's Irish. And your whiplash phrasing, like Ornette Coleman off
    the stars.

I just like thinking of you riding the Second Avenue bus
schlepping kids' clothes, groceries, slips of paper with this
    fragment or that dream
a poet's eyes on the world floating by—

the office building where Planned Parenthood used to be,
the bland yet ugly, modernist Episcopal Church,
the dull gray high-rises, a Synagogue, seemingly empty

the skinny boys carrying guitars weary from drink and doubt.
But this is my Second Avenue. Circadian, humbler, noisy,
and full of mysteries unraveling. Yours is different.

Your Second Avenue is more home, no mystery, just the late
supper needed fixing or another poet in town to entertain
between mothering and marriage and raving metaphors to be tamed.

My Second Avenue is for checking in and checking out,
away from the wrench of too many other hungry babypoets
angling for the teacher's glimpse, the mentor's tease.

It is a Second Avenue of bland buildings and skinny boys
    dangling guitars
and the phrases of Frank O'Hara, something planetary and
    there is no
Howard Da Silva look-alike on my bus. Just the usual mutterers
    and weary

ones ready for television and a really good soak.
When next we meet, it will be good to gossip about friends,
    prizes, and not our woes.
Fog contours. Sunbursts clarify grids and girders. Tower and Bridge.

Give my regards to *Tour Eiffel*. Its twin, the Brooklyn Bridge,
    makes memory
easier to hear. Those footfalls across the East River walking away
    from Manhattan
across Brooklyn, the Atlantic, on to the tenth *arrondissement*.
A café, some wine, and your laughter.

Sculpting the Head of Miles Davis

for Raul Acero

Secure the base
So the flesh will have something
To cling to; wrap wire

Around the wood and
Fill with clay, liberally;
No, continue to add

Clay—more than it seems
You will ever need for his
Indented cheeks—and slap

More onto the base of the skull;
Don't forget the constellation
Of bones in the skull;

Don't get hypnotized
By the eyes; gouge your fingers
Into his sockets—we'll deal with this later.

Pull back and follow the rhythm
Of the jaw line, rub your thumb
Over the forehead; stab

Your fingers into his cheekbones;
Raise them higher.
Doesn't his face

Cast ribbons of shadow?
Doesn't he have cavernous
Dimples? But don't make him

Smile; imagine the teeth are behind
The sheet music of his lips;
Imagine the tongue is aflame

Behind the teeth; imagine
There's a voice scratching in the throat.
No. The temples sit too high;

The nose will not bespeak
His middle-class air;
Raise the forehead,

Straighten the nose bridge,
Deepen the furrow of his brow.
Now, remember the look

In his eye back in '89 when
You saw him play at the Beacon Theater?
Can you see it yet? Stand back.

Tell me if the man whose face
You hold in your palms
Could see his mute drop from his horn,

At the *start* of his solo, pick it up—no
Lowering of the head, no shrugging of the shoulders—
And go on to blow a phrase that still

Trembles between your fingers.

HÉDI KADDOUR

The Old Wife

translated by Marilyn Hacker

He wants to have
The operation but
He's crazy
The doctors are
Crazy and then
Raising her voice to
The heavens she told him
Never!
He just needs simple
Cucumber compresses
A lot of love
Anyway if he dies
She'll kill herself.

Hail to the Artist

translated by Marilyn Hacker

In the country, he talks to her about art
About love, about life, he says that he creates
And he loves, she says that his painting
Is rubbish, he says that art is life,
She says that he's a layabout,
He plays at pricking her with a blade of grass, she
Squeals, he says he'll spank her to calm her down,
She calls him a paint-dauber, he grabs her neck
With one hand, slaps her with the other, he laughs, he says
The children can see, he lets her go and then
The next day from the riverbank he watches
Her swimming with her eyes closed, says to himself he's
As happy to be with her as he was eight
Days ago, in the same place, but with the other one.

Mercy

And this time when she asks,
The world will end, won't it?
a black river of crows will be rowing out
above you, heavy oilcloth of wings
working over slanted roofs,
dark tents of sycamore.
She will tilt her small head skyward.
So that watching her, you could almost glimpse
the secret greed of time itself,
while her question hovers, unanswered
in the slight wind of the stars' procession.
Is she remembering that evening, driving home?
How she sat beside you, singing,
and just ahead, the cars suddenly
slowed, miles of red taillights gathering
behind the frail wall of five people
standing in the fast lane of the freeway,
trying to protect something
you couldn't yet see. And then you did.
Inside the half-circle of their bodies, a motorcycle
flung against the guardrail, someone
kneeling in the thickening dusk.
Someone draped in a blue bedspread.
Because you felt it then, the past so full
of silence, and waiting.
Mercy as it comes, suddenly, or not at all.
Did she take your hand?
You had to keep on driving. Slowly.

TIMOTHY LIU

Visiting My Mother's Grave

Something's kept me away, perhaps
an all-too-familiar voice laced with
paranoia streaming through a phone

unhooked from its cradle, dangling
in that empty room. Hanging up
not an option. Her ashes in an urn

for the third straight year and now
I wonder how it was I never could
get through to her. Yet here I am.

In Hot Pursuit

across the Passaic's asphalt drawbridge into the heart of Kearny—
my cheeks flushed with wine—you the muse I did not choose
dragging danger down in chains across the hangdog face of me

as I followed you upriver, wanting you to cleanse me like a sari
fitted through a virgin's wedding band—why else would I cruise
across the Passaic's asphalt drawbridge into the heart of Kearny

still hot on your brand-new tail?—yes, you—my spanking Jersey
princess with a papa's pocketbook good for nothing but booze
and chains of smoke you'll drag across the hangdog face of me

until I cry myself to sleep in the priest's confessional, unworthy
of your whorish looks and your windows down blasting blues
across the Passaic's asphalt drawbridge into the heart of Kearny

with a fifth of Maker's Mark sloshing in your lap more empty
than the gas was ever gonna get when I got through—win or lose—
love but a daisy-chain dragged across the hangdog face of me

until crush felt more like crash upside another tab of Ecstasy
hurled overboard with seatbelts coming loose and pairs of shoes
spilled across Passaic asphalt straight into the heart of Kearny
where danger dragged its tread across the hangdog face of me.

Matins

At last she decided to speak to the moon.
Having no other choice, she begged it
to set her free. Why me, she asked,
when others are content
to sit on their haunches all night
peering at your sullen face; or feel
your granite pull beneath skin
and obey, opening wave upon wave.

When no answer still came
she decided to make, instead, an offering
of herself: stars burning on her cheeks,
her limbs entangled in sheets,
her words in the darkness formed
an opalescence, a crescent of light.

Self-Portrait in Summer

The day threatens its hold over me, the storm closes in
on the lake though I've heard it before, we've begun
with the moon. Plainly stated with my silver pen:
I wait for the day to fill me, to make its choice.

I spin myself smaller; listen, I will not tell everything.
With eating comes hunger and its enormous demands—
the tangled vegetable garden, Grandfather's black umbrella.
A space, simply waiting, agreeable to birds and windows,

sand and glass. And what I've held most dear? It falls away,
my father falls again, and I have stood behind. I meant
to catch him, but I am too small. I have waited in rain
that is nothing like love. It is like rain, and like rain,

falls straight as the house fills with its sound. Words can't help
my father; his voice is gone. Truly. But for you, I'll begin
with eight prescriptions in a glass fingerbowl, a phone call
that changed something: course of a day, course of a life.

I can't live up to lofty claims, but here I am at seven years old,
showing off my dress and beads and teapot dance.
I will not borrow pain or rage: this time, my father's wedding ring
cut off his circulation. That's all. My parents are familiar

with emergency rooms. It depends on the day, on the doctor
    and the light.
I would like one word that doesn't measure anything
but someone has already said this so beautifully
what doesn't our world leave to be desired?

My mother washes her hair, arranges flowers in many new rooms,
arranges furniture in front of walls my father has fallen into.
To this room of people I've nothing to say, so I remain silent,
or more simply, don't go. Someone walks in the garden,

the wind carries voices: a man and his small family cut peonies,
then pull a green wagon through the woods, the woods that hold
a large angel carved from a tree—true, true—and two rows
of beech trees, straight and breathtakingly tall.

GREGORY PARDLO

Winter After the Strike

You believe,
if you cast wide enough

your net of want and will, something meaningful
will respond. Perhaps we are the response—

each a cresting echo hesitating, vibrant with the moment
before rippling back.

But you're steadfast as Odysseus strapped to the mast, as you were
in '81 when Reagan ordered you back to work. You were President

of the union local you steered with your working-man's voice,
the voice that ground the Ptolemaic ballet of air traffic to
    a temporary stop.

You used it to refuse to cross the picket line I walked
with you outside Newark International.

I miss sitting beside you at the console when you worked
graveyard shift in the tower. Mom and I visited with our
    sleeping bags.

I could see the dark Turnpike for miles, the somber
office buildings winking insomniac cells, the tarmac

spread before us like a picnic blanket and you, like a jade Buddha
suffused in the glow of that radial EKG.

You'd push the microphone in front of me, nod, and let me
    give the word.
I called all my stars home, trajectories bent on the weight
    of my voice.

You say you miss tracking those leviathans, each one snagged
    on the barb
of your liturgy. I, too, get reeled in by the hard, now rusty music
    of your pipes.

I follow it back to the day of your accident in the story you tell:
you were sixteen, hurdling the railings dividing row-house porches

from one end of Widener Place to the other to impress Mom.
I imagine the way you cleared each one like a leaf bobbing
    on water, catching

the penultimate, the rubber toe of your Chuck Taylors kissed
by the rail, upsetting your rhythm and you roiled in the air
    headlong,

arms outstretched, stumbling toward the last like one hell-bent
or sick to the stomach. The way you landed, on your throat,
    the rail

could have taken your head clean off. Since then, your voice issues
like some wartime communiqué: a ragged, typewritten dispatch

which you swallow with your smoker's cough black as a tire
spinning in the snow. That winter after the strike,

we were so poor you sold everything but the house. Tell me, Dad,
when you'd stand at the door calling me in for the night,

could you hear me speaking to snowflakes falling beneath
    the lamppost?
Could you hear me out there, imitating you imitating prayer?

Tight Line

There's no bobber at the surface. Nothing
between you but trust in dumb suck
on rubber boots & faith's rusted buckles sunk
into mud banks. Eyes trained on the current
backed up against itself

like a row of empty boxcars. Nylon wound
around an index finger, stand ready for a tug come alive.
When a blood-yoked sunrise turns over on a thorn
in a bullhead's belly, you remember bushy-head, Question
Boy with the split eyebrow, who told us

where his brother buried a Hefty bag full of books
from France. & how, tethered like mildew-stained pages,
the running-downhill feel of sable smooth mystery
pounded thru us. Who was it showed Little Rock
his daddy's black

& white Polaroids of his mother? Who taught him, one
by one, to swallow lighted matches so he'd remember how
many toes he had on his shoed foot? A slowness in
the corner of your eye, a muddy V moves
& webbed claws part the surface. Is this after that

fateful day in science
class? Insects & the exoskeletal. How song-sweet & Chicago-soft
a hard boy is on the inside. Remember how the line plumbed
when big boys marched the river with broom-handled sucker
spears? Or the twins, heads like comedy & tragedy

with silvered shovel-chins
poised to dig. How one held their prized fish
so the other could go in its mouth. How about the old

man's cane pole & convex stump top? Said he lost the right
half of his behind to a Sergeant at boot camp, the left

to a foreman in the Mill. Purple fingers twirled a slipknot
into a leader, nobody's business, said he knew the bottom,
root from gnarl, of the river by his heart. When asked, said scaling
a white bass felt like scratching its back. When not, told us how
he'd never been snagged,

& how, back in Arkansas, he knew a woman
used black cat eyes for live bait & moonlight
for pocket change. The V goes under, you hear him again,
bites down on the line: you ever hook yourself
into a steady rock that moves upstream, might as well cut it loose.

The Woman Who Allowed Light
to Have Its Way with Her

She remembers
an absence of blue
billowing down,
playing loose with her,
the impetuous sailor
her mother warned her against
time after time. The light
did not invite her to dance,
nor shine upon her only.
In countless borrowed rooms
she swallowed
its gleaming intimations.
Later, in the dark, she lies
on the bed, recalling
the silvery edge of its breath,
like birch trees in spring.
She sparkles with shame.

Cutting Hair

She pays attention to the hair, not her fingers, and cuts herself
once or twice a day. Doesn't notice anymore, just if the blood
starts flowing. Says, *Excuse me,* to the customer and walks away
for a Band-Aid. Same spot on the middle finger over and over,
raised like a callus. Also the nicks where she snips between
her fingers, the torn webbing. Also spider veins on her legs now,
so ugly, though she sits in a chair for half each cut, rolls around
from side to side. At night in the winter she sleeps in white
cotton gloves, Neosporin on the cuts, vitamin E, then heavy
lotion. All night, for weeks, her white hands lie clothed like
those of a young girl going to her first party. Sleeping alone,
she opens and closes her long scissors and the hair falls under
her hands. It's a good living, kind of like an undertaker,
the people keep coming, and the hair, shoulder-length, French
twist, braids. Someone has to cut it. At the end she whisks
and talcums my neck. Only then can I bend and see my hair,
how it covers the floor, curls and clippings of brown and silver,
how it shines like a field of scythed hay beneath her feet.

Picking Up a Job Application

A spring wind hustles hundreds of pages into the street,
discarded leaflets like pieces of a shredded textbook
under the feet of high school students let out for lunch.

A young woman bends and grasps a flier: sliver of promise,
passport to enter through the golden arches, gateway to the west,
up escalator to immediate opportunity, and prosperity somewhere
higher, those sky-reaching towers across the river looking down
    on her
and the crowd scrambling to buy a dollar-forty-nine-cent
    special meal.

Required? Just the have-a-good-day sticker on her backpack,
the smiley face plastered over her eyes and nose and mouth
    every day.
And one thing more, of course: *Fill in application on the reverse—*
English only please. She speaks Hindi, Arabic, Tagalog, Spanish,
Greek, half a dozen other tongues hide behind her smiles. The day
she says *Hello* to her first customer is the day she says *Hello*
to the other women behind the counter, who are talking, but
    not smiling.

KEVIN PRUFER

The Fall of the Roman Empire

When the lights go out on a peaceful evening, it is wartime.
Who pulled the switch? Sometimes
                        all he heard was water
on sand and even the shiplights flickered off, the bulbs
swaying emptily on their poles.
                    The bombers always rose
from the horizon invisibly after dark.

He dropped a glass of wine. A bloodied handprint
on the sand. The boats sighed on their mooring,
their fine wood scraping the docks.
                    He didn't think
any bombers were coming.

*

Gracie and Earl and James. Paula and Wilson. A cloud
fell over the town and into his lungs. *Blow wind, blow,*
he was singing,
           but couldn't remember the words.
Some of his friends at their windows looked to the sky
for bombers. Some in the fields, hands crooked or splayed,
faces damp from rain.
               There was no one to bring them in.

The beach was lovely at night, as though he had never seen
a falling bomb.
            Lawndart, dropped bottle, bad word.

Never seen one tilt into the sand, but heard them
grumbling on the distant islands.

*

When Rome fell, the Romans never knew it. No one burned

the buildings down.
                    Weeds, of course, in the Forum.
A roof and no one to clear the tiles away.

Not like a bomb, not like a president. Not like the market,
ratings, the cost of gas. A sun kept rising. The same old gods
laughed up their sleeves.

A woman stopped for the night in a ruined farmhouse,
laid her mat, and slept.
                    Her brooch slipped into the rubble
so she could not find it the next day.

*

Dew collects at the eyecorners and slides down the face
when one is dead in a field. Of course, the eyes don't see.

The lights went out in town
                    and nothing to look at, anyway.

The bombers were unimportant to the passed away,
                                        his friends
who remembered a Christmas long ago, a shrill wind
scattering snow beneath the door and into the living room.

*

Such snow, his mother said, sweeping it with a broom into the
corner, then blocking the space under the door with a towel. He
looked up from his book. The room smelled of pine and hearth.
It was a book about the fall of Rome. A wind laughed over the
house
        played its little fingers on the chimney so sleepily and trim
that he would close his eyes on the sofa in front of the fire, he
would put down his book, and, although it wasn't time for sleep,
he would shut them, his eyes, his book, shut them away.

*

Some of them may have thought it. It was centuries ago.
A few, perhaps, in ruined temples. A few, in their boots,

beneath the standards.
Five soldiers straggled back into town,
grieving and tattered. Illyricum, Parthia,
the wrong side of the Danube.
A bit of dirt in the duffel,
strange implement, beer.

More birds in Rome than people. Some couldn't help noticing
the sparrow that came to rest on the arch of Trajan,
how it did not move all day
then, during the night,
just vanished.

*

Rome died. A Christmas, long ago, he had been reading about it,
and now, how strange the words were. *Alaric,* like a catch in the
throat. *Honorius,* the smooth ache in the back of the mouth. And
his wine spilled and his friends in their rooms looking for
bombers. His friends in the fields, streaked with dew.

*

And then it rained and he jogged back toward the villa,
dropping his wine on the sand.
He had had too much.
The waves came in and in, and, from far away,
the throb of an airplane's motor.

How strange when it came low over the beach,
and he fell into the brush, cupped his hands over his ears.
A whistle
of bombs. Unbearable. The tall grass swayed
around him, touched his cheek. Such an itch.
Such snow,
his mother had said. *Such snow. See it coming down, so gently?*
Into the woods. Over the Forum.
It was a beautiful snowstorm,
they all agreed. Such a crash and a roar. Into the lap of god.

SHREELA RAY

One Way of Looking at Thirteen Sailboats

Way out on the horizon—
on the thinnest blue line
sail thirteen sailboats
with white sails.

And all of them bear
the name of one woman
sailing out thirteen times
out of lives and sight.

With her faith in hurricanes
and alcohol and the Coast Guard
off-duty for the day, this time
she may be lucky.

Cruelty

The furrows deepen on your forehead
as you watch the TV story of Chief Joseph.
Later, as your amber eyes—two villages,
fade into the darkness, I deliver
a knockout without mercy,
"Does marrying me make you feel good?"

Some have been known to bob up with
"Somewhere in my bloodline is a Cherokee."

Your sad voice answers me,
I still believe in the democratic process—
and you disappear and cover the darkness.

Song of a Woman Feigning Sleep

There is nothing more than a painted room
and I, a painted woman in it
by an open window, a brass sun
and a blob of flowers on a cabinet.
Crowds come in every day to look
at the bold brass color of the sun,
the window quite unlike any other;
the cabinet with flowers.

They also look at me feigning sleep.
It's true I elicit no desire
wherever desire is to be felt by them.
It's the artist's skill they admire
for the dark voluptuous flesh.
My parts are disproportionate.

I see too well with these slit eyes.
That man is not so really brave. The fair
young girl in the white cotton dress
sneaks a look at my pubic hair.

I long for the emptiness and shut doors:
to rise and fling the windows wide
to the moonlight streaming in and to dance till sunrise.
Aster, anemone, Marigold, bells explode;
and the brave iron knight on his rare
iron horse, the woman reclining in a chair, listen.

Just before sunrise the moon goes brass.
The flowers reassert themselves as a blob.
If there is a change it is perhaps
in a finger covering a little more breast
and the bells returned to the cabinet.

The room is never more than a painted room
and I a woman painted in it.

Jairus

So, God takes your child by the hand
and pulls her from her deathbed.
He says: "Feed her, she is ravenous."

You give her fruits with thick hides
—pomegranate, cantaloupe—
food with weight, to keep her here.

You hope that if she eats enough
the light and dust and love
which weave the matrix of her body

will not fray, nor wear so thin
that morning sun breaks through her,
shadowless, complete.

Somehow this reanimation
has cut sharp the fear of death,
the shock of presence. Feed her

roast lamb, egg, unleavened bread:
forget the herbs, she has an aching
fast to break. Sit by her side,

split skins for her so she can gorge,
and notice how the dawn
draws color to her just-kissed face.

Flesh

At night the earth's flesh shifts,
which makes the house sigh
in its sleep, which sends a shiver

through the wood-bones of my bed,
which makes me stand up
in my dream and climb a hillside

flush with gorse and may.
I lie down on the peak and feel
the *kick-punch-kick,*

and wonder what the world's
child will be like—a newborn
island, steaming

with its own volcanic power,
violent and beautiful,
with empty orange skies

and seas too hot for fish,
a land that teems with flightless
birds dragging their iridescent

fans through black dust,
breaking in their voices with cacophonies
of courtship and alarm.

Morning comes, but no news
of the birth, no new islands
in the archipelago.

The world's child is lost among us,
unversed in our languages,
walking the streets with a bowl.

The Good Times Are Killing Me

It's hard to stop looking for something without simultaneously giving up hope. I don't know how. Buddhists learn the art of nonattachment, or they say they do. But have you ever seen a Buddhist lose his car keys? I have, and they're just like the rest of us.

Now that I was in my thirties, being single was entirely different. It meant candid discussions with a date, both of us saying, "Naaaaah..." but friendly-like. It meant peeling singles out of my wallet, splitting the tab exactly down the middle. I'd forgotten all my exit lines. I'd lost that Good Morning Vietnam feeling. I just wanted a little peace.

Two things told me I was getting older: last Christmas, three people gave me tree ornaments. And second, when my friends described the men they wanted me to meet, they listed their qualities. "He's an individualist, losing his hair but in a good way, Harvard grad school, wants children..." It felt like shopping, shopping blind. It used to be that we all went out, drank a jug of wine, and woke up the next morning to see what had happened in the night. These days, you go on a date with a pen and notepad. They're job interviews.

"That's why I believe dates should be conducted in a formal office setting," said my friend Jack.

Shouldn't it feel natural, spontaneous, like falling out of a tree?

Other people think I've made a mess out of my life, but I disagree. I think that I've just been efficient. I've managed to cram a lifetime of mistakes into a span of ten years. I'm still young, thirty-two, and I'm watching other people take their time with it, sticking with husbands or wives who won't have sex with them, won't clean up after themselves, whatever. I had done all that. Somewhere along the way, I'd gotten selective. My condoms had dust on them. I wanted a mail-order prince. Either that, or nothing.

"Here I am, baby," Jack said, thumping himself on the chest. "Prince Charming."

"Prince Alarming," I said.

Every time I went on a first date, the next morning I bought a ten-cent feeder goldfish from the pet store and put it in a giant jar that used to hold pickles. I named the fish after my date. I didn't give him any advantages. Instead of distilled water, I used tap water—over-chlorinated, radioactive. I did not change this water. I did not feed the fish. If my date called and the goldfish was still alive, I went out with him again. If the goldfish died before he called, I gave up on him.

"It's Darwinian," I explained to Jack.

Jack said, "That's totally crazy."

I said, "When it comes to dating, you have to be a little crazy to be sane, because a sane person would go crazy."

"Jesus. Feed it, at least."

My instincts are always wrong, but I follow them, anyway. I read somewhere that you can find your way out of any maze by touching the wall with your right hand and following that hand wherever it leads. Eventually it will lead out into the open air, even if it takes a million billion years.

Jack said I was just looking for someone whose metaphors matched mine. He said I should give up, I'll never find that, because my metaphors are stupid.

I suspect that my problem is this: I have never been able to tell the difference between longing and love. This, Jack says, is my dysfunction.

"There *is* no difference," he says.

Jack and I went to the gym and got on stationary bikes. Jack said, "This is ridiculous. A stationary *bike*?"

"It's cold out, though," I said, beginning to sweat.

"I'd rather freeze," he panted. But he kept pedaling next to me.

I met Jack five years ago at a party. He got down on a knee and said, "If I don't take you home tonight, I'll never recover." But the way he said it, looking over my shoulder and nodding at someone he knew, told me that he had said this before, maybe as recently as last night, and he had recovered quite well, considering.

Jack is thirty-five. Jack is attractive. But I say that grudgingly, because with Jack, you do. He has dark brown eyes and they change expression so rapidly, talking with him is like watching television. It's like watching television, anyway.

When he was sixteen, Jack lost his twin sister in a party-related drug incident—he won't discuss the details. She had an extreme allergic reaction and died. Jack spent the next three years at home in Tucson comforting his mother and father; then he left and didn't go back again, not even for Christmas, which he spends with my family each year. My family adores him. They think it's cute when he says grace at the table, and we all humor him, shouting "Amen" or "Hallelujah" afterward.

Unlike me, Jack had a religious upbringing. He and his twin sister were forced to take two hours of religion classes every day in school, K through twelve. One day, Jack's third-grade teacher spotted him daydreaming and asked, "Jack, why do we worship Jesus? Why don't we worship, say, you?" Startled, Jack said, "Not enough people know me yet."

Enough people know him now, but I'm his only follower. Jack and I had settled into a friendship over the last five years that had flowed seamlessly out of his come-ons. Every now and then he threw out another one, but I handled them like dents in my windshield, swerving my head for the clearer view. We were each other's oral historian, always calling to record every little event in our lives: that our ficus plant wasn't doing well, or that the guy at the gas station had shortchanged us by five dollars. Sometimes I got confused and forgot what I had told Jack versus what I planned to tell Jack, and it took us some time to iron out those details.

At the very least, it was nice to have a compatriot. There at the gym, I slid over a retro seventies postcard I had just bought next door. It vibrated on Jack's machine. It was a picture of a smiling blond woman curled up on a couch, watching her date croon a love song to her, his open mouth wide. In a cartoon bubble over her head, the woman is thinking: "The good times are killing me." Jack laughed, pedaling faster.

I told him about the date that had inspired the purchase. I had gone out the night before with a man who told me, "I'm not religious, but I'm very spiritual."

So I said, "I'm not at all spiritual, but I'm deeply religious."

He asked, "What religion?"

"Oh, you know," I said, waving my hand. "Any of 'em."

"I see we have some differences," he said.

There at the gym, Jack explained. "He was just trying too hard, that's all."

"Oh."

Jack told me about his last date, a woman who described every other man she was currently seeing, in tortuous detail. She knew how much money each man made. She asked Jack, and then repeated the number back to him to make sure she had gotten it right.

Jack had met her at a dance club where she had written her phone number on his stomach in red lipstick. He sweated too much at the club and by the time he got home, he was missing a number, so he tried number combinations until he reached her. She didn't remember who he was, and it took him an hour of all his funniest jokes to convince her to go out with him. He said that the date had gone so poorly because he had used up his best material on the phone.

My legs hurt. I looked at the exercise machine, unable to decipher it. "Help me with this thing."

Jack leaned over and punched some buttons. A drop of sweat fell from his forehead onto the panel. The pedals got looser. I stared at the sweat shimmying on the plastic as I said, "I don't know why you're even bothering with her."

"Because she doesn't want me. Once she changes her mind, I can leave her alone." He wiped his forehead with his arm and glanced at me.

"You always go after unavailable people."

"If the available people were all that great, they'd be unavailable," Jack said.

"Not true."

"Yes it is."

"I refuse to live in your Tom Cruise world," I said.

But was he was right? Don't you live in the world you're stuck with? I mean, I never wanted to live through two Bush presidencies, but here I was, saying it again: President Bush. And here we were, Jack and I in T-shirts, pushing some pedals around. That night, we'd each go on a different date. We'd call each other the next day and complain about it. He'd tell me something like how, during sex (and there would be sex), his date said, "*Hup* two three four..." and I'd tell Jack something like how my date said he was only interested in women who could ski.

When do the stories end? Is that why people get married, and why married people are so boring? Because you marry the guy who will give you no stories to tell? Is that what I wanted? No more stories?

Jack created a "Chicks I've Nailed" database. When he disclosed this information over lunch, I said, "Never tell this to another woman."

He said, "Eleanor. It's a wonderful introspective tool. For example: although I *say* I like hippie chicks, the plurality of girls I've slept with have been artsy types."

"Oh my God."

"I'm just trying to figure out what I'm doing wrong. I printed out a pie chart..." He started groping in his bag.

"No. Put it away."

"But—"

"No."

Jack was working a new job doing sales and marketing in the building next to mine downtown. He said that he had taken a two-thousand-dollar pay cut for the convenience of seeing me. Of course, I didn't believe this, but we did have lunch almost every day, like now. I picked up my sandwich. Jack did the same, but just held it in front of his mouth while he talked.

"This is what I'm so sick of hearing: 'I really like you, Jack, you're a great guy, *Jack*. But I just don't feel that spark with you.'"

"Oh. Nice guy syndrome." But he wasn't a nice guy, so I didn't get it.

Jack put down his sandwich without biting into it. "I want to figure out this 'spark' thing. And control it."

"Don't you think you're missing the point?"

"I want to gently open my hand and see a little flame in the center of my palm, dancing." He stared at his hand.

"On the prowl again," I said.

"That sounds a little more...real than I'd like it to," Jack said, finally eating, mouth full. "I'm on a mission. I have a list." Jack flashed me his list, maybe twelve women long, with phone numbers next to them. Some had question marks instead of last names. One woman he simply called "Satellite Girl." He kept the piece of paper on the table while he talked, explaining that he had finally, seriously considered what he wants, and who fits the image. He wants the big, big love, composed out of an aggregate of characteristics. I peeked. Halfway down the list, I saw my own name.

I had a big love, once—Richard. The way it started was this: I had met Richard at a bar and was instantly smitten, but he didn't notice me. One day Richard called for my roommate Pete, who wasn't home. When I answered the phone I was lying on my bed, playing with a stone a geologist friend had given to me. She had explained, "See the shiny parts? See how it's kind of oily-looking, chipped in weird places? Long ago, a dinosaur ate this stone and kept it in its gizzard with other stones to help digest its food." Sometimes I tried to put it in my own mouth, but it was too big.

When I knew Richard was about to hang up I said, "You'll never in a billion years guess what I have in my hand."

Richard paused then bit, asking questions. Is it old, new, pretty, ugly, what color, what shape? When I finally told him, he asked me out. We were in love for three years, and then he fell out of love abruptly and left me for a woman who makes bagels.

Despite all that, maybe that's what love is, after all—holding out your hand and saying, *Here. I'm holding this small, simple thing, as old as time itself. Do you want it? Is this what you want?*

Now Jack asked me what I wanted, pen poised over an old receipt.

"It depends," I stalled.

"Come on," he said. "Any nonnegotiable requirements? Any personal habits you can't stand?"

All I could think to say was that I didn't want a man who picked up his plate in restaurants and licked it. Not like last time. Jack wrote, "No plate-lickers." He stared at the paper for a minute and then said, "Well. I think we can find you something."

We both looked up suddenly. The woman at the table next to us had just started crying. "Michael . . . that's . . . so . . . ," she said, her cheeks turning red and wet. "I tell you I have feelings for you and you just laugh at me like that I can't believe you made me say that stuff out loud when you don't care about me I feel sick I'm going home."

Her chair screeched back, and she rushed away, shoving her arms into her jacket sleeves. The man, Michael, stood up, threw money on the table, and said, "Ellen, wait! Ellen!"

Ellen did not wait. She pushed her way toward the door.

Then, in a voice probably meant to be just loud enough, but overcompensating at the last minute when he realized that he was losing her forever, Michael boomed: "STOP! ELLEN! I LOVE YOU! TOO!"

Ellen stopped and turned around. They stared at each other across the room. Nobody moved. The place fell silent. Even the music stopped, stuck between songs.

Someone called out, "Kiss her!"

Michael walked over to Ellen. She looked up at him. The music began again, an accordion winding through the melody. A voice sang in another language.

They kissed.

People cheered.

Michael and Ellen kept on kissing, as if they were alone, as if the world were whirling around them in a hurricane, and they were caught right in the middle of its beautiful blue eye. Then they walked toward the doors, holding hands. This, what we were witnessing, was the extraordinary beginning of something ordinary. Or maybe the other way around, I don't know. Strangers smiled at each other. A little boy started laughing. A woman reached across the table to hold her husband's hand.

Jack and I stared at each other, then at the lists fluttering on the table as the double doors opened and closed.

I had to drive down to Colorado Springs for a meeting. On the drive back I was hit with a freak spring blizzard, almost a white-out. Peering through the shooting snow, I saw a solid black billboard on the highway with giant words in white: "WHO'S THE FATHER?" Sponsored by an adoption agency. I wondered how many pregnant women drove down this highway, suddenly snapped their fingers, and said, "Come to think of it, who *is* the father, anyway?"

Waiting for Jack that night, I threw part of a leftover bagel into my new goldfish's jar. It sank slowly and rested on the bottom. The fish stared at it.

It was still snowing when Jack drove me to a party at his friend's house. In the parking lot, he combed his hair with the brush end of the ice scraper before we went inside.

We took off our coats in the hallway. Jack looked at my outfit and made a cat noise, deep in his throat. I didn't know men could make cat noises.

"Nice skirt."

It was tight, made out of old neckties sewn together. I said, "Thank you."

Jack ushered me inside, saying, "I need a girl exactly like you. Except maybe with lower standards."

"How about her?" I asked, pointing with my head at a girl in a silver tank-top and a gold miniskirt. I could remember times when I felt that desperate. The girl was smiling at Jack. He said, "She's a sparkly."

"She's pretty." She had a big red nose. She looked like she was terrified that nobody would talk to her all evening. She held a glass of wine by the stem with one hand and caressed the rim with the other. She meant to be suggestive, I'm sure, but instead it was just vulgar. I wanted to wrap her in a big fireman's raincoat. "She seems nice, Jack," I said.

Jack moved so close to me, I could smell his soap. I looked at his left shoulder as he whispered above my ear, "I don't like her, um, breasts."

"What?"

"They look bitchy."

I looked immediately at the girl's breasts. Maybe it was the power of suggestion. They did seem somewhat bitchy in her silver tank-top, like they were gossiping together. Even though I was staring directly at her breasts, the girl's eyes passed right over me and on to Jack. She slowly walked toward us.

Shouldering me aside, she asked Jack to dance without even glancing at me. He took her in his arms and maneuvered between laughing and drinking people, guiding her in a pretty two-step. I settled back to watch, next to a random couple by the seltzer water and pretzels. The couple was arguing loudly. It's hard not to listen, especially when you can:

Boy: Hey. I'm sorry things didn't work out between us. I just don't want the closeness.

Girl: The closeness? I mean . . . Jesus. People need people.

Boy: Not me. I am alone. Without warmth. Without need.

[I spilled my drink.]

Girl, voice wobbly: Well, you have some of my things. My book.

Boy: Should I mail it to you?

Girl: Mail it to me.

Boy: I don't want to mail it to you. That's so impersonal.

Girl: Mail it to me.

Boy: Maybe instead you could come over—

Girl, voice of steel: Mail it to me, you cocksucker.

I laughed. Then I felt immediately lonely. I looked for Jack. The sparkly woman was leading him away by the hand. In passing, he grabbed me with his other hand and rumbled in my ear, "She's taking me home to show me her—" then was yanked away. He waved on the way out. He was my ride.

In a few seconds he was back again, thrusting a twenty in my hand. "Can you get a cab?" he asked, holding my shoulders and bending down to catch my eyes. "Is that okay?"

"Of course," I said, suddenly furious.

Jack landed a giant kiss on my forehead and left again. His absence seemed as absolute as his presence. I stewed, looking around. Men played air hockey in the corner, while women watched. Someone spilled a bottle of vodka and just left it there, leaking onto the carpet. A little terrier scrambled under the couch, then lit out of the room.

A blond guy now sidled up to me and slurred, "So, what's your story?" He was wearing a Hawaiian shirt with hula girls all over it.

"My story?"

"Have a boyfriend? You married?"

"No."

"Wanna be?"

"I don't know."

"Want kids?"

"Yes."

His eyes finally managed to focus on my left eyebrow. "Can you speak a foreign language?" he asked.

I excused myself and crossed the room. I leaned against the wall and nodded at the girl next to me, who was rolling a joint. She lit up, and we silently smoked it together. Then she wandered away. In a few minutes I realized that it's not rude to ditch a party if nobody notices you're there, so I called a cab and went home.

That same night, still stoned, I took off my clothes and stood in front of my full-length mirror. Did I have bitchy tits? How about the rest of me? It was a cold early spring, and my limbs huddled together. Desperate legs? Was my crotch . . .

No. No. I covered my face with my hands.

Images of my breakup with Richard flared up. Mardi Gras beads swaying from the rearview mirror as he said, *Don't love you,* the rim of dust on the speedometer, *Not anymore,* a dog crossing in front of the car and looking back at me for a long moment, *Maybe I never did,* then turning its head, following its leash, its sweeping tail the only happy thing in the world.

Nothing was worth that. I pulled the covers over my head and stayed that way until I fell asleep.

Since I've thrown away all my lone socks, their mates have returned from the sea. I hold them in my hand, thinking, *Where have you been all this time? Why can only one of you exist in a single space?*

Back in the saddle, I told myself, and went on a beautiful date with a consultant at my office named Andrew. He picked me up and took me around town, holding my hand. It was a warm spring night, and he stopped me in the street to touch my face and pull me closer. As he was kissing me, I was already wondering if he would call, his lips on my lips, our eyes closed.

Jack said, "What a loser."

"What do you mean? I haven't said anything bad about him."

"I can just tell." He picked a leaf off my shoulder and rolled onto his back on the grass. His shirt poked up an inch, his pierced bellybutton showing. The park was empty except for the two of us. "This is a new one, right?"

"Jack!" I pulled up some dead grass and threw it in his face. He blocked it with his arm and squinted at me.

"Frankly, I can't keep track of all the men you're not sleeping with," he said.

"What about sparkly girl?"

"I drove her home but didn't go inside. I kissed her on the cheek. Went back to the party, but you were gone." I stared at him. He waved a fly away and said, "She'd never pass my test, anyway. I had a feeling." I was still staring. "I didn't fucking feel like it, Eleanor, okay?"

I had the goldfish test; Jack had the Buyer's Remorse Test. It's very complicated—I don't understand it. It's a Pavlovian-response-voodoo kind of thing, involving the girl's phone number, whether or not you feel like buying new underwear, what you do when you drive past her house, and a hair sample. I don't know what you do with the hair.

I didn't see Jack all the rest of that week. Then early Sunday morning, he showed up unannounced. He banged on my door until I let him in. I was in pajamas, my hair bunched up. He didn't say a word, just walked over to my goldfish jar and picked it up. "What's his name," he demanded. The goldfish lurched around inside, bug-eyed. Stringy fish shit whirled up from the bottom.

I rubbed my eye.

"His *name*," Jack barked.

"Andrew," I said. I felt like a caught sadist.

Jack looked at the fish. "Andrew," he said firmly. He walked out with my jar, my fish, my date. The door stuck open behind him.

The next day, Jack called me at work. He was mumbling. I leaned back out of my cubicle and looked at the window, open a slit. I caught my own dark eyes in the pale reflection on the glass. It was beginning to rain, quietly.

"Andrew died, didn't he?" I said.

No sound but the start of rain on dead grass. Then, "Yes."

"He didn't call," I said.

The weather was doing its crazy spring thing. Snow, then sun, seventy-degree weather, then many days of incredible wind. Power outages and the sudden peace that they bring. I tried to fly a kite, but it was too gusty, and the kite lodged itself in a tree. Downtown, the wind kicked up, and people's white shirts simultaneously billowed out, making them look like pirates stranded far from their ships. People did strange things. As a homeless man passed by, he pointed his finger at me and said, "You just try speaking your mind in *Tehran*, missy." A woman in a pink suit stood at an intersection and sang loudly, into the traffic, "Don't Go Breaking My Heart."

Jack was also beginning to act different. He stopped telling me about his women, and he grew quiet when I told him about my latest non-adventures. He now sometimes got angry at me very suddenly, for nothing. For dropping a chopstick. For pointing at a painting in a museum. Once he grabbed my arm and hissed, "Eleanor. You are making me lose my mind." All I had done was show him a bruise on my elbow. Then he released my arm and wandered over to the pay phones and back.

One time he put his head in his arms and shook it, as if my mere presence were torturing him. I burst into tears, right there in the delicatessen.

Jack was immediately contrite, stroking my face, pulling tissues out of his pockets. Only Jack would come prepared with tissues.

"I'm sorry," he said again and again.

"I don't understand. You suddenly hate me. You pick on me."

"I don't hate you. I'm just going through something."

"What?" I asked, blowing my nose.

Jack didn't say anything.

"Why?" I pushed, sniffling.

"Eleanor. Cool it," Jack said.

"What? What? Whywhywhywhywhy?"

That night I went to dinner with my Turkish friend Deste, who had "erased" her last boyfriend and now had another. Things were going well with them, she said, because she treats him badly. "He has all these extra weights on his belly. I call him Fatty."

"Deste! He'll be traumatized."

"It's better this way," she said. "Walking in the street or out with friends, he's going to say bad things, and I shut up. But at home I say, 'I don't like the lunch you packed for me. Make it again. I don't like ham today.'" Her eyes wandered to the window. "Tonight, you will make a list of what you want…"

"Another list," I said. Apparently this was cross-cultural.

"…and think about it, all those little things. Like, I want a man who will shave his armpits. American men won't, so I want a Turkish man. So you make a list, and you look at the list every day, and *fuck* us on it. Fuck us hard. If you don't fuck us, you will never find that guy."

I stared at her. Then, "Oh," I said quickly. *Focus.* "But I want someone who makes me forget about that stuff," I said.

"That's dangerous," Deste said. "Never forget anything. Only forgive."

I looked out the window, and there was Jack outside in the street, waving a cell phone at someone or something. This often happened—he was everywhere, all the time. I was beginning to think he was actually a yogi, inhabiting more than one body at once. The lights from the buildings tinted his skin orange. I pounded on the window to catch his attention. He turned our way, but didn't see me and walked away again.

"How about that man?" Deste asked.

I was kind of daydreaming. I said, "Jack. That's Jack." Jack passed by once more, and I banged again on the glass, louder and louder, until people started twisting around in their seats to look at me. Jack turned his head in all directions. Deste pulled at my fist, but I used the other one until Jack finally walked away, stopping and looking back once as if he suddenly remembered something.

I had to go to a Saturday wedding. A coworker was getting married, and my pseudo-friend Marcy was going to be there. Marcy had married a lawyer, and I could no longer stand to talk to her on the phone. All she talked about was what her husband had fixed that week—the toilet, the patio door. She said she had a friend she wanted me to meet, named Paul. She had never been nice to me. I asked Jack to be my date.

Throughout the ceremony, Jack kept pretending to weep. The priest forgot the vows and instead made some up on the spot, insisting that Kathleen "obey" and telling Fred to say, "With this wing, I thee wed." Fred said it verbatim, teeth clenched. Jack kept trying to hold my hand, and I slapped it away discreetly, biting the inside of my cheek.

While Jack scouted hors d'oeuvres at the reception, Marcy grabbed me and pushed me over to a short, chubby man with a kind face. He breathed hard as he gripped my hand.

Marcy said, "Paul's a doctor."

Paul said, "I do medical research."

"Oh yeah?" I asked. "That's wonderful. Because everyone needs . . . medicine."

"I enjoy my specialty," Paul said, hands in his pockets so that his stomach pooched out and his hips looked a yard wide.

"What do you specialize in?"

"Mucous."

"Oh, mucous," I said.

Paul nodded quickly. A cracker crumb fell out of the corner of his mouth and onto the floor.

Marcy said, "Paul's the leader in his field."

"There aren't too many of us," Paul said, waving his hand.

"Still," Marcy said.

I said, "Where's the bathroom? Do they have a bathroom here?"

I didn't get more than a few steps away before Marcy pulled me aside, her fingers pinching my upper arm. She hissed, "I was kind of thinking you and Paul would get along. But you brought that guy." She was holding me in place.

"Jack," I said, glancing at him. He waved a cracker at me and mouthed, *The good times are killing me.* I turned to Marcy. "I wanted to bring a date. Everyone else has a date."

"But I thought I had made it clear on the phone."

"What?"

"That I wanted you to meet Paul."

"Yeah. I met him."

Jack sat down next to Paul and said loudly, "Soooo...you're a mucous man."

"Ha ha," Paul said sourly.

Marcy whispered, "I don't know, I'm disappointed. Paul's been so lonely."

"So get him a goldfish," I said. "I have a goldfish."

Jack boomed (for my benefit), "How do you get your samples? Do they use special tissues?"

Marcy said, "Give him a chance."

"I don't want to," I said.

Paul said, "I don't work with the actual mucous. I have assistants for that. I do the more theoretical stuff."

Marcy said, "You think you can be so picky, Eleanor?"

Jack said, "*Theoretical* mucous?"

We finally sat down, me next to Jack, Paul on my other side. Marcy and her nondescript husband sat facing us across the round table. We dug into our scratchy, filmy salmon and water-logged yellow squash. Jack and I drank a boatload of wine, toasting everything. The waiter spilled a glass of water. We toasted him, too. Halfway through the wedding torte (Kathleen and

Fred's attempt at non-controversial originality), Marcy smiled and said, "I'm so proud of you, Eleanor. I mean, you don't have it easy. Your life's not what I'd call great."

Oh, no, I thought.

"Look at you," she said. "You're unmarried, alone, struggling financially, you're unmarried..."

"I'm twice unmarried," I explained to everyone at the table. "Some people just do it once, but I'm an over-underachiever." Smiles shot from everyone's faces at different intervals, like bullets at a firing range. Jack glared at Marcy.

She said, "You don't have a house, you don't have any of the things we talked about wanting when we were in college. Remember? And here you are, still so...hopeful."

"Yeah," I said.

"I can't believe this shit," Jack said.

"She's a trooper," Marcy told Paul.

"I'd like to make a toast," I said, glass raised. The others raised theirs, too—it's a reflex, the way applause breeds applause. I paused. "Here's to suicide," I said. I drained my glass and turned to Jack. "Wanna dance?"

Jack stood up and faced Marcy. "You suck," he told her.

I said, "Yikes," jumped up, and pulled at Jack's arm. He hung back, staring, lower lip slack. He looked like he was going to challenge Marcy to a fight. Marcy's husband stirred, realizing that he should do something. Marcy shrank in her chair. Paul's mouth opened, food still in it. Jack took a loud, deep breath, as if he were going underwater. "You..."—we all waited, motionless—"*really* suck," Jack finished. He swayed a little.

I said, "I love you."

Jack jerked his head to stare at me. His mouth was open. Mine was, too. So I said it again, experimentally: "I love you?"

And I did. Why? Because I did.

"What kind of love?" Jack asked. His fists were loosening.

"You know," I said. "Love."

Paul snickered.

Jack just stood still for about nine seconds. Then he quickly pulled me to his chest and dipped me all the way backwards until I could see the ceiling above his head. "Really?" he asked. "Really?" I nodded, upside down.

Jack pulled me up and kissed me deeply, in a way that showed practice, forethought, and intoxication. I kissed him back, with all the ardor of my own experience. *This is Jack,* I thought. *This is crazy.* I heard some vague heckling from the table beside us. But Jack kept stubbornly kissing me until everything else faded and we were left alone with this newborn thing we had somehow created—strange, imperfect, so much better than the best of what's around.

Kudzu

On that night, years back, we were up until the cardinals started calling. The first one lit out through the leaves before the air went from warm to hot. I remember that the call sounded lonely in the quiet of early morning. But soon, just before it got light, many of them were fussing in the poplars outside Evvie's porch. The sky was turning bright behind the kudzu that was taking over the back fence. Evvie had poured more of whatever she drank with her coffee and lay lengthwise on the porch glider. Her legs were crossed in my lap. When I ran my fingers around each toe, she broke from humming to herself, and her lips pulled tight against her teeth. She breathed like the breathing was getting her off. She breathed like that when she came, hours earlier, when I had her bent over the back of the glider on her porch.

That's how she makes me say it now—*bent over, entered from behind*—like we're a coroner's report. She doesn't like it if I say *doggy-style*. When I first caught up with her today, I tried that out—just to joke, like we used to do—but she looked dead at me and sucked her teeth. *It ain't like that now,* she said, no shame in her face. Evvie tells me not to say things like *sweetmeat* and *assfuck*. She says she'd rather not talk about sex at all. But years back, when I massaged her feet, she dribbled her drink, opened her mouth, and let her neck go slack, face to the sky. Her teeth were slick with the wet of her tongue. And I figured all that had to do with me.

But there was a lot to that night. When the sun had been down a while, the sky was still bright with red and purple, like the whole dusk was swollen. The air was wet. Clouds were thick and hung close to the hills. Like early morning, those birds were carrying on. And when we first got to Evvie's place, the cicadas were buzzing as it got dark. *You know what that's all about,* Evvie would say. Even now, that buzz goes through me like an emotion, everywhere at once. It sounds like spring works: from inside your middle. By early morning we'd been at it all over the house: couch, rocker, hallway floor, twice in the bathtub.

Later, we sat in the mist as it blew across her porch. The scent of turned earth was on the air. I was thinking that the wind was horny, just like everything else in early June. Breeze blew through where the kudzu was thick enough to round the sharp corners of the fence. The wind pushed the vines from their tangle and fanned them out into the yard. When the kudzu moved like that, it looked like something large and hungry was rolling around inside. Sometimes I imagined there was something scrambling through the vines. Sometimes I was sure of it: a dog or a man, looking for some stash they dug or threw back in there. But I never saw anything, just breeze through vine. There was a hum to the breeze, a soft heave from the greenery. Above where the vines covered the top of the fence, the night was near quiet, but had a low sigh, just like that heave. And above all of that we could hear the Bensons, her upstairs neighbors, fucking again.

We listened to their couch scoot in short scrapes along the floor above Evvie's front room ceiling. The Bensons were both talkers. They made love the way they argued. He was sweetie's big daddy, she was his fat-back baby, on and on like that. Day was coming, and they were wearing out their front-room couch. We could hear them from her porch, in the back of the building. I was nodding in and out of sleep. But Evvie listened. She had her lips open, and for a moment she held her breath. In the stillness, she went stiff, and all we could hear was Mrs. Benson: *You gettin' it now, sugar. It's right there . . . get it right there!* Something splintered and shook the ceiling. And Evvie let out her breath.

When I ask her about that now, she says she was sighing back to the night air.

"I used to do things like that," she says.

"You still do," I say, like I have any idea what she's doing now.

She smiles at this, sips on her drink, looks along the bar. There's a downward turn to her lips, like whatever she's looking at in this place disappoints her. She hasn't been here for a while. Macky's Mellowtone Grill is the same as it was three years ago. Vinyl-rimmed bar and tables, six wood booths, the same color as the red that Dessa, the owner, painted the whole place. Even before Dessa took over, I never knew the inside of Macky's to have another color. It was a narrow room with a long bar. Beer signs between pictures of Booker T., Dr. King, and Garvey; Nancy Wilson above the jukebox. There wasn't a bar display, liquor bottles lit up and all that, but if you asked for something, Dessa would pour it. The jukebox never played new tunes, but stopped playing the oldest, about one album at a time. I brought Evvie by here to see the fellas, shout *Hey* to Dessa.

Evvie gets up to pick songs on the jukebox, and it's only then that I see what I couldn't make sense of when we bumped into each other earlier. She looks like she never came from here: headwrap, bangles, toe rings, and something like a sheet or a big robe brushing the tops of her feet.

"It's a *caftan*," she says when Dessa stares long enough.

"Your money, not mine," is all Dessa says.

I ran into Evvie at the barber's. I go once every two weeks. She was walking out of Willie's shop when I was walking in. The whole room was busting out in laughter. It was like she had never left Watertown. I heard her voice first, a laugh that's deep from in her chest and loose, wide-mouthed, like a child's. I expected to see her in nursing scrubs. She used to spend half her days in them. When I'd pick her up from her shift, we'd go straight to Macky's, and although the fellas saw me with her, looking like that, it didn't matter to me. She wore thong underwear underneath. *Just for you, baby,* she used to tell me. She knew I liked that kind of secret. Three years since I've seen that woman.

When I ran into her outside Willie's, I saw that caftan covering her and wondered what was under all that. Somewhere in there was her body, but when I tried to give her a hug, she didn't let me hold her long, so I got more cloth than hip. I couldn't feel if she was bigger or more bony. Before anything else I said, *Let's drink something.* We walked to the car as quiet and shy as prom dates. We were silent most of the way to the bar.

I looked at her while I was driving. She watched the streets go by. She was fanning the hem of the caftan between her knees. *Still don't have air conditioning,* she laughed out the window. *Most folks wear less when the sun's out,* I said, and she sucked her teeth, rolled her eyes, gave me that shows-what-you-know look. The next time I looked she had the hem pulled to her thighs. There was a scar of raised skin along the outside of her knee. She had been an athlete: volleyball, basketball, track; the baby girl in a house of three brothers over six feet. The knee gave out on her at regionals; the slower girl she had just beat to the basket fell on her leg. A year later, she won the Tennessee state finals for long jump. The skin around that scar ran to her thigh; her muscles were taut, like she was always ready to sprint. *It's been a while since I saw that,* I said. She was looking out the window, letting the air rushing past the car push against her palm. When she turned to me, I was trying to laugh, but she wasn't smiling.

She was the one who first got me talking that way. Hints and taunts that led to clothes on the kitchen floor and sweat on the counters. That's what I wanted to say after we had our drinks and found a booth in Macky's. Years back, she liked to tell me to tell her what I wanted to do. I tried to talk the way she wanted. At first, I wasn't that creative. We'd get a few drinks in us, and I'd push the dishes into the sink so we could use the counter. *I hope you're ready, baby,* I'd say, and when she'd say, *I've been wet since you pulled out this morning,* I would smile like a wallflower until I could think of what to say next.

As I got smoother with the smooth talk, I'd leave messages on her beeper when she was on lunchbreak, something like, *Don't be wearing nothing but oil when I get home.* I did it just for laughs. But she'd knock off work a bit early and be sitting on her front porch with a robe on and a glass of rum by the time I got there. Or I'd see a note on her screen door—*Got your message*—and I could smell sandalwood oil drifting from inside, like the whole house was waiting for me. For a while it was good like that.

Not long after, the Bensons moved in upstairs. The first time we met them, they were going at it outside Evvie's apartment. We heard them before we saw them; from the parking lot, they sounded like somebody was wrestling on the stairs to the upper floors. We walked up the steps to Evvie's door, and there they were, in the stairwell. Her heels were in the middle of the landing. We said, *Ev'nin',* and he pulled his hand from her skirt. They nodded back. He patted her ass with the heels as they went up the stairs.

They played the same record all night. Albert King on into the early hours. The Bensons were louder than their stereo. Whatever got them horny got into us, too. That night, Evvie and I almost broke her dining-room table. After a month, it was like that every weekend, two or three times on Saturdays alone. Evvie got to listening for them: if I was fucking her, hearing them pushed her to yelling herself, or, if it was sometime between the last and the next time I was fucking her, she started touching herself.

After a few weeks of that, she would put her hand over my mouth when I got to telling her how I was going to do her. *Listen,* she would say, and gaze at the ceiling. Above, Mr. Benson was making damn sure Mrs. Benson knew who her ass belonged to, or Mrs. Benson let Mr. Benson know damn well where her sugar bowl was: *No, baby, you just watch this time, watch how I do it.* Evvie's eyes would be closed, her hand over my mouth, her legs going tight, quivering into her own good time. *You just watch how I do myself.* Because they went at it late at night, we were up, too. By the time the sun was shining from the front room down the hall, we were on Evvie's back patio with the glider cushions spread out on the deck. The Bensons would be just above where her bedroom let onto the patio. Before the paper hit the front porch, we had been back in the shower and sweaty all over again on her front-room couch.

Unless they were going out for drinks, Mrs. Benson was always home, playing Carla Thomas 45's over the rattle of a sewing machine. I never did figure out what Mr. Benson did.

It got to be that we spent most nights at Evvie's. Late at night I would wake up to the carrying on upstairs. Sometimes what they said didn't make sense. Just shouting and hollering. I'd wake out of dreams and wonder what the hell was I hearing. From my dream it sounded like somebody's pet locked in a closet, but then I'd hear her say, *Got-damn, Ronnie, get it, baby,* something like that, and I'd remember what it was. I'd look to see if Evvie was asleep, and her eyes would be wide open to the ceiling. On some nights she would mouth whatever it was the Bensons said the most. When I finally said to her, *You never bust out when we get it on like that,* she said, *We never get it on like that.*

After a few weeks, I wasn't sleeping over there. We didn't argue or get cold with each other. It just seemed like more nights we slept or listened to the Bensons. Then it was more nights we either fell asleep, or I wasn't over there. Eventually, Evvie stopped calling every day, and I found myself at Macky's most weekends, watching the ball game. I told myself it was because the Braves were good that year. A few months later, folks stopped seeing

Evvie around town. When Dessa finally asked me where Evvie had run off to, I said west. That's all her phone message said. Dessa said, *That ain't too damn specific,* and I said, *That's Evvie.*

Some weeks after that I ran into Mr. Benson at Macky's. He was running nine-ball over some kid who didn't have sense enough not to bring his two-weeks' pay to a bar. Mr. Benson didn't say much more than *Which hole you want me to put the nine, son?* Mr. Benson was one of those brothers stuck in 1983: dressed sharp in leisure suit combos and two-color Stacy Adams patent leathers, blue-tinted eyeglasses, geri-curls long in back, close above his ears. Between games he'd lean into the bar while Dessa freshened up his Johnnie Walker.

I eased up, yelled to Della, *I got his, and pour me double whatever it is this brother drinks.* He looked my way, saw that we knew each other, and turned back to stare at himself in the mirror that ran along the bar. I told his reflection, *If it's the drink that keeps your lady and mine up at night, I gotta try some of that shit.* Mr. Benson tipped his glass to our reflections in the long bar mirror before he turned to the pool table—*It ain't the drank.*

After that he ran five games of nine-ball on me. He only spoke to call a pocket or ball combination. When he was done, and I had bought him a double at the bar, he tipped his glass to the mirror and smiled a smoker's yellow-tooth grin, *The lady just likes what I got and likes it a long time.* He didn't say another word, and I didn't ask anything else.

Evvie looks like she wants to go. We haven't said much: traded news about friends and laughed a little about my brickhead nephews. She gets up to put more money in the jukebox.

"The Teddy Pendergrass don't play no more," Dessa shouts. "You wore that out, Evylyn."

Evvie lets out that wide mouth laugh. She bends over, like she's going to laugh herself to the floor. Her hands go to her waist, and I can see where her hips begin. For a minute I think maybe the head-wrap and caftan are a joke and any moment she's going to throw that off and ask me to dance close, my thigh between hers, and it won't matter what's playing on the jukebox. She sees me watching. She watches me sitting at the edge of the booth, like I might get up.

"You still funny, girl," Evvie says to Dessa, and by the time she's back to the booth, her smile is gone.

We sit for a while, waiting for Dessa's sorry jukebox to find something that plays. I can hear the empty record slots, clicking, clicking. Evvie keeps her eyes to the street.

When I ask her where she's been all this time, she tells me that she's been traveling.

"I just drove," she says.

"*Drove* another brother crazy, right?" I laugh.

She isn't laughing. "Drove west. Drove north. Away from here," she says.

"Lookin' for your gold-tooth sugar daddy."

"See, that's your problem," she says. "Got shit figured out before you know shit about it."

I don't say anything to this.

"Maybe if you paid attention some of the time, you'd have some damn sense."

Now it's me who feels like leaving.

She tells me how for a long time she didn't call anybody in Watertown, or any of her kin in Tennessee. Months before she left, she took to saying *I live in Watertown, but it don't live in me.* Bars and beauty salons were the only happening places around where we lived. Beyond that, Watertown was rail yards, half of downtown boarded up, industrial parks, and neighborhoods where white folks only allowed us in to clean. Once a year, the city would put on a blues festival on Eleventh Street—five bands, barbeque, cold beer, and card games all day—and folks would almost get to thinking that there wasn't much else to look forward to. When she had enough, Evvie drove the hell out of here.

I ask her whose bed she was sleeping in all this time.

"Didn't matter where I woke up," she says, "motel, parked in a campground, somebody's couch. Nights were just me, by myself. That got to feeling good. Wasn't nobody next to me but me." Then she looks dead at me. "Whose bed was I in? You mean who was I *fucking*. You really got to know that?" And then she told me more than I wanted to know. At first she was using her fingers. Then she tried some toys. She took an art class, made something out of clay, thick with ridges; it had a curve to it, and she thought that was like me, but after a while, she said she didn't need it.

Threw it away in a Waffle House dumpster.

She made her way farther south than Watertown. South, she says, just south. Maybe it was in Georgia where she found a way to stay in somebody's house for a while. She didn't say if they were kin or not. Just a house in the middle of trees and heat. She would walk the swamps, gig for fish, gather wood. She didn't say how she paid for things, but after some months, she burned her scrubs and nursing shoes in a trash can.

"Thongs, too," she tells me, like that's the part I should laugh at.

After all of that, I try to lighten things up. When I ask Evvie who she's fucking now, she doesn't answer right away. She sucks her teeth again, pats her head-wrap, looks at her hands.

"I didn't have no place or nobody. I had my car key, *one key,* on my chain for a whole year," and when she says *chain,* there's a drop in her voice like I haven't heard since she called 4:30, some Sunday morning, early in the first year after she left town. She had her drink on: loud, sassy, sloppy. In the background, I could hear a car engine rumbling. Maybe it was a truck. I could hear wind blowing like it came from some cold as hell place. She was yelling at me. She'd go on for a while, and I'd try to say something to calm her, but I didn't try to say all that much. It was 4:30 in the morning.

In the background, I could hear some woman laughing a sludge-thick smoker's heave that begins with a chuckle and ends with that shit they never hack up. It seemed to me that this woman knew Evvie. *Fuck that nigga, Evylyn,* she kept laughing. I couldn't tell if she was laughing at me, like she had me figured, or just laughing at Evvie, drunk on the phone and yelling at some man in Tennessee. She probably had that figured, too. I tried to tell Evvie to call me back when she was alone. She told me she was getting free of her chain, all those nowhere brothers. When I asked her what did all that have to do with me, there was a silence on the line. I could hear her breathing hard against the cold where she was. After a while, I hung up.

When Al Green comes on the jukebox, I say, "That's my jam," and I get up to get us more drinks. From the bar I watch her mouthing the words. She looks out the window, to Eleventh Street: folks walking from downtown, home to work, brothers gathered outside the bar, shit-talking about last night's game. She lets her head bop a little, a small sway of her hand back and forth in the air, like she's a backup singer. The song fades, and she's still looking out the window. I stand at the bar longer than I should, but she never looks my direction. Dessa comes from behind the bar to have a smoke. She's looking at Evvie, too.

"What did you do to that girl?" she laughs.

I don't know what to tell Dessa. Last time I thought I had Evvie figured out, cardinals were calling.

The Statues

One morning the people of the capital awoke to dozens of bronze statues: in front of parliament, a horse and rider both the size of Great Danes; behind the concert hall, a waif in a tutu on a tree stump playing a huge violin. In the library lobby, a creature with a low forehead, protruding teeth, and hairless paws, a cross between a cocker spaniel and a warthog. The Queen, it seems, had cast enlargements of the miniatures on her dressing table.

It was rumored that the statues contained secret cameras, and that a royal eavesdropper had been appointed to monitor conversations. In protest the citizens tied balloons to hats and gave the warthog sunglasses; they placed mounds of chestnuts below the rear ends of horses.

The philosophers found a lesson in irony. The doctors wondered if the Queen was senile. The artists, of course, hurt most deeply. Surrounded by such ugliness, how could they teach beauty? But the people learned to live with the statues—the Queen had, after all, put bread on their plates—although there was a precipitous rise in both melancholia and glaucoma. It was like living with the sound of a cracking whip. Did the Queen know, the people wondered, that when she died, the statues would be melted into a coffin for her, with her body like a ladybug inside a tuna fish can? It would take an entire regiment to carry the bier.

Graphology

Whenever she met someone, she secretly analyzed their handwriting. She wondered if these insights were illicitly gained, like wiretapping, but reasoned that graphology was merely close attention to the person without the distraction of interaction. Each element of the psyche had its equivalent mark on paper: the dominant upper zone of one friend indicated spirituality, the crowded letters of another, greed.

Every so often she analyzed her own handwriting. She trained herself to write in the way she wanted to be read: her capital "I" was simple and direct, her small "d" showed creativity without affectation, her spacing suggested generosity and good will, with a sense of social boundaries. At one point she saw her lower zone getting smaller and she made an effort to be more sensuous.

Another time she noticed that the distance between her lines had increased, indicating isolation. Someone she loved was slipping away from her, like a fish in a stream of water. But she did not know, until she saw her splayed fingers, that it was she who had let the fish go.

The Philosopher's Name Was Misspelled Everywhere

Man is the cruelest animal. She wanted to sleep with the philosopher, she wanted to feel the warmth of his back against her chest. Some people had trouble with the consonants, others reversed the vowels. He made her think—that was his gift. She wanted to name a restaurant after him, the offerings cued to his epigrams: Bellwether Pie, Christian Vice Pudding. *The abdomen is the reason why man does not easily take himself for a god,* he had said. She was always hungry but she knew words wouldn't feed her or save the Tutsis in Rwanda. When she thought of genocide, she wished she could lose her appetite. Of course he'd been dead longer than the million Tutsis who had been macheted into pieces. A low-tech war. Unimaginable, she would have said, a hundred years after the philosopher's wisdom: the savage appetites of ordinary people turned to killers turned back to ordinary people.

Orpheus Plays the Bronx

When I was ten *(no, younger*
than that), my mother tried
to kill herself *(without the facts*
there can't be faith). One death
or another every day, Tanqueray bottles
halo the bed and she won't wake up
all weekend. In the myth book's color
illustration, the poet turns around
inside the mouth of hell to look at her
losing him *(because it's not her fault*
they had to meet there): so he can keep her
somewhere safe, save her place
till she comes back. Some say
she stepped on an asp, a handful of pills
littered the floor with their blues,
their red and yellow music. Al Green
was on the radio. *(You were*
at school, who's ever even seen
an asp?) It bruised her heel
purple and black. So death
could get some color to fill out
his skin, another bony white boy
jealous of all her laugh too loud, her
That's my song when Barry White
comes on. He's just got
to steal it, he can't resist
a bad pun, never never gonna give her
up, or back. The pictures don't prove
anything, but one thing I remember
about the myth's still true:
the man can't live if she does.
She survived to die for good.

How People Disappear

If this world were mine, the stereo
starts, but can't begin
to finish the phrase. I might survive
it, someone could add, but that
someone's not here. She's crowned
with laurel leaves, the place
where laurel leaves would be
if there were leaves, she's not
medieval Florence, not
Blanche of Castile. Late March
keeps marching in old weather,
another slick of snow to trip
and fall into, another bank
of inconvenient fact. The sky
is made of paper and white reigns,
shredded paper pools into her afterlife,
insurance claims and hospital reports,
bills stamped "Deceased," sign here
and here, a blank space where she
would have been. My sister
said *We'll have to find another
Mommy.*
        And this is how
loss looks, my life in black plastic
garbage bags, a blue polyester suit
a size too small. Mud music
as they packed her in
damp ground, it's always raining
somewhere, in New Jersey,
while everyone was thinking about
fried chicken and potato salad,
caramel cake and lemonade.
*Isn't that a pretty dress
they put her in? She looks so
lifelike.* (Tammi Terrell

collapsed in Marvin Gaye's arms
onstage. For two hundred points,
what was the song?) Trampled
beneath the procession, her music.

Pieces of sleep like pieces of shale
crumble through my four a.m.
(a flutter of gray that could be
rain), unable to read this thing
that calls itself the present.
She's lost among the spaces
inside letters, moth light, moth wind,
a crumpled poem in place of love.

The Absence of Light

God works in mysterious ways, Father said,
but He's not half as mysterious as your mother.
He said, Let there be light. And there was light.
I don't see anything mysterious about that.
He did what He said He'd do.
Your mother says, Let's not be late for the movie.
Yet she takes so long getting dressed
that it doesn't pay to go. Then she
gets mad that I don't take her anyplace.
God created light where there was only darkness.
She only creates confusion.

SANDY SOLOMON

Packs Well

"Packs well," she says, forming in ungloved hands
snowballs, lopsided, roughly made, and calls
her big-boned shepherd and my scruffy mutt
to catch each high underhanded toss.

They make us laugh as they leap to mouth midair
those cold nothings. A chew, swallow, or spit
and, ready for the next gift, they sit to watch
her dig and palm. Sometimes she rises from her crouch
and throws long to make them run to the spot

where snow meets snow again and disappears
into itself. They circle, nosing, tonguing
winter's traces—no smell, no taste, no sound.
Only feel and see the world, chill
and simplified now, except on the rise

where that blue round of sled the children guy
to the top, that disc on which they crowd (blur
of proximate color and sound) starts down,
turning as it glides. And falls, again, apart.

Small Deaths

Still slight under heavy folds of pleated smock,
she swells with talk of midwives, queasy mornings,
while he changes the subject, changes the subject
as if by pulling the other way he could stop

the drift down her chosen path. Each seems to shrink
in the sure, clear flame of the other's want
as the talk, like oxygen, shifts back and forth,
and their faces, strained with want's denial, adjust.

Like them we contrive our lives in "compromise"
for love's uncompromising sake. How soon
must *we* two wonder how we might have changed
if choices abandoned had been the choices made?

The Owl

I imagine he's sitting nearby
like a Sufi on a roof, hollow-eyed,
   intense, burning at midnight.
Something snaps. He has learned
   the art of breaking, & being broken.
His call is naked as a needle, sharp
   as images he sorts from afterimages,
arranging them like flames. In the pines
   he echoes off stone walls, blue snow.
Bones turn beautiful under his gaze.
   His voice makes you want to quit
your job & go somewhere far away
   that may never have existed,
but you want it, for what doesn't
   exist can exist always. Then
he is just his sound fading,
   calling as if only to himself,
waiting if he answers, & moves on,
   perhaps trying to catch up.
When he's gone you don't know
   he's gone, or if he was ever there.

The Star

You're writing down next spring's
   garden: beans, tomatoes, squash
& so on. Outside, snow sticks everywhere,
   clogging everything up, hemming

You in. When done you pick up
   the newspaper. In the obits
there's always someone you know.
   They come & go, & you never

Quite get used to it. Walking
   slowly downstairs you call
to your wife: How about a game
   of cards? O.K. She shuffles, deals,

Lifts her head. Look, she says,
   That huge star. I've never seen
anything like it before. It looks like,
   who knows. You turn & see it,

Whiter than snow, harder than fire.
   She lays down her hand, goes
to boil water. Imagine, she says,
   what a star like that must be.

Imagine, you say, already
   at the North Pole,
gazing steadily,
   forever.

Widows: A Section of the Law Books

what about their celibacy?
widow playing maid for an in-law and
if high-born inheriting three thousand   not more
shaving her head
wearing only white   I do not know
this law   lying on my lord's burning branches
I do not mind getting old
my forehead creases   though
my mouth still turns up
I love trying on dresses even when
          I give them all away
I love buying them back new in my fictions
the pink one with paisley swirls and the red
border at the v of my neck
yes he could die or change the course of my boon
yes he could pack up tomorrow
and I could hold sorrow on me   a cold stone
loss of god
tea leaves drenched on a saucer   yes
it is better
not to entertain breaches
and I do not know what equals adultery

I Never Had an Imaginary Friend

I would've called him Ice Cream, or Monopoly,
or Grand Slam: something I especially liked.
He'd have played catch with me when no one else

was home. He might have come from planet Fev,
where God taught him kung fu. He might
have traded crescent kicks with Christ. Or been a girl.

Maybe on Fev, boys and girls weren't shoved
apart by the snarling referee Propriety,
when all they wanted was to clinch. My friend

might not have been human. He might have had
two heads, or wings and scales, or tentacles.
He might have been a brain floating in a jar,

a pulsing blob, or a rock who saw the future
and, by thumping, told me what to do. Maybe I did
have such a friend, or many, before adulthood's

German housemaid scrubbed the memory away.
Maybe everything was my friend in those days:
the grass that left green blessings on my pants,

the baseball glove that couldn't wait to hold my hand,
even the sun which, when I went shirtless at the beach,
stared at me with so much love I burned.

Nola

—main character in Spike Lee's film She's Gotta Have It

How many nights I have lain in bed
thinking of you, Nola Darling.
I climb the fire escape from two floors below to see you
soaking your stained panties in the sink,
frying your liver and onions.

I have seen you naked in the bathroom,
raising my eyebrows at the secret of your stretch marks.
Watched you scrape the calluses away,
pluck the forked eyebrows,
shave the legs, thighs, and chin.
On Sundays, I expect the smell of texturizer,
wet heat in your hair.

I trail you to the supermarket,
know your weekday list well: lemons for your iced tea,
mango (fresh or sugared, for a treat),
bread, fish to fry, and salad dressing—if it's on sale.
Once, two years ago, you were short a dime
for a pack of gum and yogurt on your way to work;
I rescued you, the silver sweating with my hunger.

Nola, Nola, Nola.
Devil's floozied mistress. Hot, panting stray.
I could never take you home to my mother.
I would have to send you to wardrobe,
call in makeup, shine the soft lights liberally
to sop up the oil of your seduction.

Inside your little space,
I've watched a humble church rock
with a congregation of one, sometimes two,
your bed a sinner woman's pulpit,
your body an aisle for conniptions.

O bronze heifer, do you think of me and my yearnings?
Everything you do seems for someone else.
Soon, I will be bold enough
to climb through the window,
wearing nothing but my boots
to trod your hidden wet funk.

You'll fight me, won't you?
Your monstrous hands will throw me down,
you'll laugh, and I'll see the silver fillings
in the back of your mouth,
taunting riches to run my tongue over.

And I've brought the wine,
white, and strong enough
to cut through black memory.
Dissolve the rough edges, make you safe for me.
Tonight, I own this free stink spiraling into the city.
I ride your bed of candles,
lapping the cork off your skin,
the bright red from your lips.
Pull the scarf from your head.
Relish you.

Bitch, I have seen you choose randomly.
Who I am doesn't matter.

Assimilation

Already at work—squatting, preening—
the Cambodians weed the cranberry bog.
They're close to the earth like mourning doves

foraging below the bird feeder—the last to come,
to take what others dropped. There's no moaning.
They're chatty, a giddy cackle carries among them

while they move together. They're alive as the frogs
that ga-dung in the ditches. Faint yellow clouds
of pine and oak pollen slip down, coat them.

The expert on their boombox calls it a natural response.
To what, it's not clear. Every bright surface dimmed,
subtly altered. The crew boss swings by

in a new midnight-blue van. He's traded in
his wide-brimmed straw hat for a baseball cap.
He oversees. He squints at his own kind.

Walk Right In

All summer and fall the couple floats hand in hand from work at the shelter workshop. Hand in hand in their secondhand sleeveless oxford shirts. With target tattoos on their deltoids. Even in the winter, the same way, hand in hand, although bundled up in secondhand wool coats. One snowy evening, right after they pass by like this, Jack, a regular at the bar which nightly watches the couple, says that he's heard they claim to hold hands even when they sleep, and this way stay aware of the other's dreams. "They can even enter each other's dreams if they wish," Jack says. They *are* nuts. Bizarre; ridiculous claim. And for what purpose—true or not—would one enter a dream? That's the kind of conversation that ripples the bar till the barmaid, Louise, says, "Because they could change it. They could walk right in on any dream gone sour and turn it around." And that puts an end to the debate with a total hush. Except one bitter night about a week later the couple walks right in, pulls up chairs in the lounge, and sits holding hands beneath one of the barely used, cozy round tables. His rotten and her chipped teeth chatter. They refuse any offers to drink to get warm. The longer they sit, the place turns creepy, somber. Realizing this isn't good for anyone's business, Frank, the bartender, finally shouts, "Then, what the hell do you want?" "Our bed," the man says. "I can't wait to get home and climb in. And sleep. Sleep." "Okay, come on," his partner says, hauling him up by his coat sleeve, tugging him toward the door, "it's time to get home." She pushes him out, and in the entrance turns around to address the bar. "Thanks for letting us get warm for a minute. We didn't mean to bother. Sorry, too, about Mike. He does a good job at work. He's a good man. Sometimes he gets a little upset when he thinks he's not getting anywhere." Her thick, out-of-date glasses make her eyes wide as dolls', and because, after she speaks, the whole bar almost falls in, they think, *She's warming up, getting ready, once Mike's asleep, to go in, straight up his arm and into his head so to set things right.* Right after they're gone, Frank buys a round of drinks, and Jack, who claims he knows all about them, starts up with, "I hear Mike takes advantage of her." Wouldn't any one of us here? the bar thinks. And before another debate stirs and ends there, it's silent.

AL YOUNG

Up Jumped Spring

for Nana

What's most fantastical almost always goes
unrecorded and unsorted. Take spring.
Take today. Take dancing dreamlike; coffee
your night, creameries your dream factories.
Take walking as a dream, the dearest, sincerest
means of conveyance: a dance. Take leave
of the notion that this nation's or any other's earth
can still be the same earth our ancestors walked.
Chemistry strains to correct our hemispheres.
The right and left sidelines our brain forms
in the rain this new world braves—acid jazz.
The timeless taste her tongue leaves in your mouth,
stirred with unmeasured sugars, greens the day
the way sweet sunlight oxygenates, ignites
all nights, all daytimes, and you—this jumps.
Sheer voltage leaps, but nothing keeps or stays.
Sequence your afternoon as dance. Drink spring.
Holding her hard against you, picture the screenplay.
Take time to remember how *to get her* spells *together.*
Up jumps the goddess gratified; up jumped spring.

With Rhyme and Reason

Your John Wayne days and ways are on the wane.
Who needs another gangster, when this world
is jammed with gangsters, brilliant, slick, insane?
You whose thing is you've been boyed and girled
and worked and played, then turned and stretched and squashed.
What's with it with you anyway? Ideas
you spew about your innocence have washed
up on the shores of all the bottled fears
you've sailed with notes inside: as tunes, as film,
as yarn, as poems; some hero swaggering
through or to some hell, some mythic realm
(or not so mythic realm). How staggering!
You talked your sleepy stuff, you swindled time;
you sold moon rocks, you set up all your own
brain-children, Humpty Dumptys. In the slime
and slow romance of infamy, you all alone
did all the dragging, drugging like John Bull
did way back when he ruled. Your Uncle Sam
just couldn't bring it off, didn't have the smarts.
Where Sam freaked for the buck, a quilt, some jam,
old John, your master, ushered in the arts.

Famous Builder

In a deep socket of an empty acre lot in South Jersey, a wiry boy with dark eyebrows, burnished blond hair, and thick lenses in his glasses is clearing pathways through the milkweeds, trying to preserve as many of the leafy, muscular stalks as he can. He's working harder than he's worked in weeks, so hard that he doesn't even hear his father's car engine in the distance, or his mother ringing the cowbell for him to come inside for dinner. This is Telegraph Hill. This is the first community he's built that he's genuinely proud of, from the curving of the cul-de-sacs as they wind through the woods, to the discrete street names he's penned in meticulous, Early American script on scraps of faux-antique wood he's pilfered from his father's workshop: Saybrook Road, Weston Drive, Lavenham Court, Henfield Road. No wonder his fingers are cracked and cut, his toes sore from using the front end of his sneaker as a tool.

The wind rustles the weeds. He's about to back up the slope, to look out over his first fully-wooded community, his belief so deep that he can practically see the lanterns trembling on, the hushed couples stepping up the sidewalks toward The Northfield, the most recent two-story model (vertical rough-hewn siding, copper-hooded bay window). Then Tommy Lennox, his neighbor, is walking toward him with a football tucked beneath his arm, the faintest suggestion of a smirk around the corners of his lips. "What's that?" Tommy says.

A ripple, a blush to his skin. The boy's pleasure's been so private, so intimate, that he might as well have been making love to the land. He can't even raise his eyes. "A development," he says finally.

He's heating up inside his shirt. The boy imagines Tommy stepping through the community casually, knocking street signs aside, crushing the tall can that stands for the silo at the entrance. Sweat runs cold across his back. But when the boy finally lifts his head, he's surprised to see the animation in Tommy's face, the quizzical expression that suggests he's waiting to be shown around.

In no time at all, Tommy's building his own development, Willow Wood, in the open land beside the single pine along the back of the lot. He's out there every day, just as the boy is, digging with his mother's garden shovel, replanting tablets of moss until the knees of his pants are soaked through. But why doesn't this feel right? The boy doesn't have the heart to tell Tommy that he simply doesn't have the gift for this, that straight streets intersecting at right angles went out with 1949. And what to make of the names Tommy's assigned to them: Motapiss Road, Vergent Court. They practically carry an aroma, suggesting all sorts of things no one likes to talk about: flesh, death, the mysteries of the body. At least Tommy's sister has the good sense to know that she should pay attention to what's attractive. Though Cathy Lennox's Green Baye is entirely misnamed (what bay? what water?), the boy cannot help but be impressed with the added *e,* and with the skillful way her streets meander down the slope.

Still, neither of their projects can stand beside the elegance and understated good taste of Telegraph Hill.

Today all the neighborhood children are roaming the field, some down on their knees, others carving out streets, all squinting, foreheads tightened in concentration.

The boy looks up at the houses across Circle Lane where he and his friends spend their time when they're not in school or out here. Of course it would be their misfortune not to live in a real development, but in a neighborhood in which all the houses are decidedly unlike each another, with no consistent theme: Dutch Colonial, French Provincial, California Contemporary. Though his mother tries to invoke the word "custom" as often as she can, he's not having it. Most of his fifth-grade classmates live in the newest developments, places where the wood-plank siding's coordinated with the trim (sage-green with aqua, barn-red with butter), always that pleasing sense of order and rhythm. How he frets about living in a place with no name. Oh, to say "Timberwyck" or "Fox Hollow East" or "Wexford Leas" and be entirely understood. His dilemma even seems to bewilder that substitute teacher with the kind face and the gray, washed-out hair in whom he confides one day.

"You don't live in a development?" she says. "How could you not live in a development?"

Flushed, he turns away.

"Have you talked to your parents?"

He shakes his head. He steps back from himself, watching: Silent boy, ghost, so weightless and emptied he barely has a body.

What would she say to the story *The Philadelphia Bulletin*'s just written on him: *Boy, 12, Longs to Be Famous Builder*? He imagines her unfolding the newspaper at her kitchen table, spreading orange marmalade on a burnt piece of English muffin as her teakettle whistles on the stove. Would he be real to her now? Though it tells of the six hundred brochures he's collected from developments all over the country, and of the fan letters he's written to Bob Scarborough, whom he wants to work for someday, it frustrates him, if only because it's written in that cheerful, yet patronizing tone that suggests his work is mere play, that he'll come to his senses in a few years. Hard not to wince when he sees it tacked to his principal's green bulletin board. How he hates being on display like that, lying on his stomach in the photograph, marveling at that brochure in his hands (is it Charter Oak?) as if he'd never seen one before. He'd like to tell the substitute it's an ineptly written piece, a foolish piece, but he's as guilty of the lies as anyone. Why did he simplify himself when he talked to that reporter, why did he allow her to think there was something less than profound about the binders of street names he'd collected? Here he was, hiding the ferocious depths of his passion inside something harmless and benign, when all he really wanted was to move her, to show her he was in love.

When he looks up from his reverie, both Tommy and Cathy and all the others are wandering back toward their houses, the sky charcoal above the rooftops, the trees.

He gets down on his knees. He shivers inside his jacket, which he zips, chucking the skin of his throat, but he'll work long after the streetlamps have blinked on, defying his mother's cowbell, ignoring his long-division assignment, the piano scales—all those dull, grinding duties that suggest his life has nothing to do with pleasure, the warmth of this soil in his hands.

Native Sandstone

There was no house yet, just a wellhead where the house would be, under an overturned box to keep the sand out. Clay was building the house, and it would be one to live in for a long time, so they were trying to get everything right. From the passenger seat, Susan watched him wedge the box between the green metal stakes that kept it in place. He climbed into the car and threw the water sample into the backseat.

"Now," he said, and he sat with his hand on the ignition.

"The sandstone," Susan said. She checked her watch, hoping they wouldn't interrupt Albert's dinner.

"Right."

Clay backed the station wagon out onto the flattened grass of the road, past the bare area where the well-digging rig had pulled up all the vegetation. Susan got out and dragged the barbed-wire gate aside, and shook the dust out of her sandals before pulling her feet back in after her.

"So, you'll ask Albert," she said. They drove out on the empty two-lane highway. "You always know what to say to him."

"What's to know?" Clay said.

The wind grew louder through the open window. "I just mean he trusts you," she said. Albert was eighty-three, and he had welcomed them warmly—unlike some of the locals—without suspicion of their intentions; he said he thought the town could use new blood. He liked Clay's photographs and always asked Clay about his picture-taking.

"I wonder if we should take him something," Susan said. "Something he could use." She tried to think what that would be. Not a book; he didn't read. He had read the dictionary page by page growing up on a farm, waiting for the wheat to grow, and he knew all the words, but he said books with stories made him tired. Maybe sheet music; he played guitar in a bluegrass band called the Catfish. A retired ethnologist played banjo and mandolin, the local plumber played fiddle. But she didn't know anything about bluegrass.

"Albert gets along all right," Clay said.

Behind them the water sample rolled to the other side of the car with a thump as they turned off the highway. Susan flipped the visor mirror down to see if there was dust on her face, and pushed her hair behind her ears. Her skin had taken on the color of the desert bluffs, she thought, wrinkled at the corners of her eyes. Clay seemed to be moving in the opposite direction: in spite of the gray in his hair, he looked younger.

They pulled up past Albert's irrigated peach trees and parked between his sky-blue '65 Ford truck and a washing machine missing all four sidewalls, so only the top and the guts remained. A pile of cut sandstone from the pioneer days, chiseled by pioneer hands, spilled down a slope into the rice grass and knapweed. Susan scanned the pale red blocks, wondering, not for the first time, how much exactly there was, how much might be buried in the lawn and under the visible stone. The stone had once been a schoolhouse. On a pilgrimage to the library in Blanding, Susan had looked up an old sepia photograph of boys in caps and girls in aprons standing before a tidy one-room structure with a peaked roof, the blocks held together by mortar now long eroded.

Clay went first up the porch steps, his hair flattened on one side from camping on the property, his two-day beard speckled with white. She followed, conscious of their empty-handedness, their lack of an offering when one should be made. As Clay pulled open the screen door to knock, he said, "You ask."

"You'll help," she said. Then the door opened.

She was shocked by how much older Albert looked. A padded white brace over his shirt held back both shoulders but didn't keep him upright; he bent at the waist as if to make up for the straightness of his braced spine. His eyes, behind thick glasses, were watery and gray.

"Albert," Susan said, trying not to sound too alarmed.

For a long, awkward moment at the door, Albert seemed not to recognize them. "You're back in town," he said finally, and he gestured them in. He moved a pillow to make room among the song books and music catalogs on the couch. Under the pillow, the floral blanket covering the upholstery was torn.

"Guess that's in disrepair," he said, and he sat on a folding chair at a card table stacked with opened and unopened mail. Susan tucked her skirt under her knees and sat on the edge of the easy chair.

"I fell last week," Albert said, his hand on the thick white padding of the brace. "I was on the phone long-distance, and I started talking—saying words that aren't words. Words I was making up. And then I fell backward and lit on my shoulder." He unbuttoned the top two buttons of his shirt and pulled the fabric off his shoulder, revealing a bruise the color of a black plum from his collarbone halfway down his left arm.

Susan flinched at the sight of the bruised skin, and regretted it. "Oh, Albert," she said.

"Some people were here, I had some people visiting," Albert said. "I don't remember what happened, but they got me to the hospital."

"Do you need anything now?" She wished they had brought something useful—a loaf of bread, a quart of milk—wished Clay were acting even a little sympathetic. The accident was going to make their request difficult. Albert was not what he had been.

"I still cook up big soups like when my brother was alive, so I've got stuff in the freezer," he said. He spoke to Clay, who flipped through a book of bluegrass songs.

Clay closed the book in his lap. "Can you play guitar still?"

"I haven't, but I can play," Albert said, fingering chords in the air with his left hand. "If I could rest this elbow on something. Are we supposed to be playing somewhere?"

"I don't think so, not until you're healed up," Clay said. "The band needs you."

"Well," Albert said. "Yes, I have milk and everything." He waved a wrinkled hand with flat, calloused fingers in Susan's direction. "When my friends came by they brought me milk."

Susan tried to think who the friends would be. "The friends who took you to the hospital?"

Albert looked at her. "I was on the phone when I fell, I was alone."

Susan glanced at Clay. "I'm sorry," she said. "I thought you said friends were visiting."

He stood, frowning, and rummaged through the papers on the card table. "Well, people were here," he said. "I wasn't stuck on my back like a turtle all night." He hobbled, bent over in his brace, into a back room.

Susan whispered to Clay, *"Poor Albert."* She felt like the vultures that soared over the valley in the afternoons.

"Can't find the date the Catfish are playing," Albert said, returning. "Losing my memory. Just ask in town."

There was a pause while he sat back down at the card table. Susan wasn't ready to abandon their purpose, but she did wish Clay would ask. Men turned to Clay, they trusted him. He did what he said he would; that was why she had married him. But he also held to what he wouldn't do; he had said, *You ask,* and he was sticking to it. She edged forward on the easy chair.

"Albert," she said, trying not to sound like she was trying to sound as if it had just occurred to her. "We were wondering about that sandstone in the front yard, if you'd be willing to sell it to us."

Albert looked at her and said nothing.

"I mean, if you want to get rid of it, we'd take it off your hands," she said, with a little open-handed gesture and a shrug.

"The sandstone," Albert said, and he turned to Clay. "Have you talked to Kyle Yazzie lately?" he asked. "Is he going to help you build your house?"

"I think so," Clay said easily, moving the bluegrass book off his lap. "He'll lend us his backhoe, anyway."

It was always the way, she thought: Clay got to make breezy conversation about gear and tackle, and she was stuck with requests and complaints. Kyle Yazzie was on the Navajo tribal council; Clay and Albert would start agreeing about him in a minute. He was a man men liked to agree about.

"You should dig up a garden plot while you've got the back-hoe," Albert said.

Clay looked to Susan.

"We're not planting much," she said. "Just desert plants we won't have to water." She was embarrassed; she felt strongly about water use and native plants choked out by imports, but she didn't like to proselytize. And she knew Albert liked his lawn, and liked the imports; he said Russian olives made good shade trees. "I think we'll grow some peppers," she offered.

"Kyle's a nice young man," Albert said. "Plays a good banjo, too."

"His kids have been out to play on our land," Susan said, cutting off Clay's agreement, and feeling foolish once she had done it. She liked Kyle's boys, who chased each other shouting through the tamarisk. She liked his shy daughters, too; the girls were pretty, and she wondered when they would stray from home, and where they would stray to.

Albert said, "Kyle was helping me with some paperwork, a couple, three weeks ago. I guess I trust him all right. I can't always see the numbers." He shuffled magazines and bills around the card table. "Well, I guess I'll give you that sandstone," he said.

Susan said, "Oh, we'd want to pay you for it."

"It was the old schoolhouse, you know, when the town was settled," Albert said. "It was cut from the massive sandstone around here." He gestured at the bluffs outside the window with the back of one hand. "They built that schoolhouse before they built the church. I always thought the schoolhouse must have been prettier than the church. I never thought it was a pretty church, even when I thought I might get married in it."

The thought of Albert in a morning suit in the boxy Mormon temple made Susan want to laugh. He wasn't a Mormon but didn't dislike them; she had seen him argue genially with two boyish elders at his door. "Who were you going to marry?" she asked.

"Oh, no one in particular," Albert said. "I just thought I might." He said it to Clay, who smiled as if he understood.

"It was a pretty schoolhouse," Susan said. "It's beautiful stone. We want native stone to build with, railroad ties, things that fit in. We thought before we cut new stone we'd look for some that was already in blocks."

Albert stood up to look out at the half-buried stone. "When my brother and I, he's dead now, when we bought this place in '66, that stone was there," he said. "We built this house that year, had it built. I still have things to finish, like the molding on that door." The front door was unvarnished, covered with yellow sticky-note reminders; the doorjamb was painted Sheetrock.

"Works fine like it is," Clay said.

Albert dropped his weight back down in his seat. "I'm eighty-three, I'm probably not going to finish it," he said, and he looked at the back of his hand on the card table. "Those stairs still need to be carpeted. My brother was going to do that. Other things he was going to do." He stopped. "Yes, okay, I'll give you that sandstone."

"You don't have to sell it if you don't want to," Clay said. "Susan just wants a house that's *authentic.*" He grinned at her, and she frowned.

Albert said, "My brother and I were going to build a house with that stone in '66 and had this built instead. Let's call it tentative. When do you need it?"

"Not till spring, I guess," Susan said, calculating. She didn't want to give him all those months to change his mind, but she had a guilty sense they should give him as much time as he wanted. "We can get it anytime."

"Okay. Tentatively, you can have it." Albert pressed lightly at his bruised shoulder. "I want to think a little more."

"No problem if you change your mind," Clay said.

The three of them walked out on the porch and looked down at the pile of rock.

"We could come get it tomorrow or wait till spring," Susan said, fearing suddenly that Albert would forget the conversation and someone else would take the stone away. The people who brought the milk, or the ones who took him to the hospital—if those were, in fact, different people. "Whatever's best for you."

"*Tomorrow?*" Clay said, looking at their station wagon in the driveway. "I don't know how we'll ever get that stuff out of here."

"Clay's building the house, so we're not on any schedule," Susan said from the porch stairs. She said it lightly, to cover her misstep. Of course they weren't ready to get it tomorrow.

"With me building," Clay said, "we might never be ready."

"I'll think some more about it," Albert said. "I won't sell it to anyone else, let's say that. Other people have asked for it over the years, but I always thought I'd get around to using it." He pointed out in the yard. "Look, quail," he said.

A covey of eight birds ran out in a line from behind one of the peach trees.

"The ones with quotation marks on their heads," Susan said. The birds marched toward the tamarisk, seeking cover. "I don't remember what they're called."

"They live out there. I hear them all the time, their call is like this," Albert said. He looked hard at the planks of the porch for a few seconds, then whistled a three-note call. "It sounds like, 'How *are* you, how *are* you,'" he said. "And the answer is like this—" He paused again and whistled.

Susan laughed. " 'I'm just *fine,* I'm just *fine,*' " she said.

Albert smiled at her. Clay shook his hand. Susan walked down and leaned over one of the stones in the yard, hands on her knees. Other people had asked for it; they were not the first. But they were the most current. They had the first yes.

"You can see the chisel marks," she called up. "It's not enough for a house, but maybe a wall."

"A foundation," Albert said to Clay on the porch.

"Oh, we don't want to hide it," Clay said. "We want to see it."

"Always thought I'd do something with it."

"You could put some more peach trees in where the rock pile is. I'd help you plant them."

Albert turned from the stone to look at Clay for a moment, his hand across the white brace on his chest.

"You still taking pictures?" Albert asked.

"Yep," Clay said.

Susan said, "You come out to our place when you get more mobile. And don't fall down anymore."

Albert smiled. "Don't plan to." He took off his glasses to clean them on his shirt.

"Think of a price if you decide to sell it," she said. "I don't know how much a rock costs. If we could even have a few of them, that'd be great."

"Well, maybe we can work out a trade," Albert said to Clay.

"Sure," Clay said, and he started down the steps.

"We'll think of something good," Susan called, one hand on the car door, the other shading her eyes from the low evening sun.

Inside the station wagon, Clay started the old engine. "How am I gonna move those blocks?" he said. "Low flatbed trailer, I guess."

"Easier on the chassis," Susan said, and they both were silent. The car was hot, the light no longer pleasant but flat and oppressive. The engine seemed loud as they backed down the drive.

"You wanted it, too, right?" she asked.

"Sure," Clay said. "Just don't know how I'm going to move it."

"You weren't much help," she said. But he'd done all right, and anyway they had the stone. "It almost didn't feel worth it," she said. "I thought he knew he wouldn't use it."

"You want to give it back?"

"No. Someone else would just take it."

Clay turned the car around in the clearing by Albert's toolshed, and the water sample in the back rolled again to the other side of the car, bumping against the door. Susan looked over her shoulder to wave goodbye, but Albert didn't see her. He stood against the porch railing with his glasses in his hand, straight-shouldered in the brace and tilted forward, staring out at the spilled and overgrown jumble of stone, the peach trees beyond, the red bluffs across the river.

Susan took the water bottle in her lap to stop the irritating thumping, then looked out the windshield, away from Albert. "Are you sure he understood?" she asked.

Clay nodded and ran a hand over his rough beard.

"If we think of something really good to do with it," she said, "then it won't be so sad to take it." She closed her eyes and found she couldn't picture the stone as part of a building, only as free-standing monuments on their undeveloped lot, upright versions of the ruin in Albert's yard. A bathroom wall with places for soap and plants but without a bathroom, a garden wall with no garden. With effort, she held those walls steady and added a frame-work around them, a roofed house between the shower wall and the garden. Windows and a door, stucco, visible beams; she constructed the house until they reached the two-lane highway, the stone supporting ceilings and turning corners in her mind.

Fictions

1.

I am my father's sidekick, Mutt to his Jeff, Costello to Abbott, Tonto to the Lone Ranger. I am his pal, his fall guy. I follow him like a shadow. He calls me "Me Too." Sure there's a comic strip character named Me Too, but I am too young to know that. I fall into the name. "Me Too," I say whenever my father puts on his overcoat after supper, announcing in this gesture that he will walk across the street to the candy store where he'll buy a package of Lucky Strikes, stand around or sit at the counter, and drink a cup of coffee. This is the world of men, and I want to be there, sitting on a stool next to my father, sipping milk through a straw, and spinning around inside their voices. The house where we live has a small hallway where I stand, clutching the rough wool of my father's trouser leg, tilting my head, and looking up the long length of his body. He looks down, and he teases. "Hey, Pip-squeak. Hey, Runt. Whadda ya want?"

He knows, of course. Still, I do what I have to do, beg and plead. "Please, Daddy, please, take me with you. I'll be good. I won't ask questions. I promise."

He laughs, ruffles my hair, then signals my mother. "Get her coat."

My father is tough, and he's smart. He smokes cigarettes; he plays cards, poker and gin rummy. He places bets off the track. One day, when I am five, my father stops a runaway horse. We're driving to the Jersey Shore, stopped in traffic the way you stopped then, cars bumper to bumper on the white-hot highway. Other cars have pulled off the road, and they sit, hoods raised, radiators overheating and leaking steam, whole families sitting beside them, faces glum. The sun beats down. It's hot outside, hot in. My mother fans herself with her hand. Chrome glints. My father leans over the wheel. He talks to himself. He talks to us. "I can't understand it. Why don't they move? I'm telling you, never again, so don't ask."

I'm the one who pleads and whines, the one who wants to build castles in the sand, to swim in the ocean, walk the Boardwalk, eat cotton candy, ride the rides, then play the wheels of fortune with my father and Grandma Rose. I kneel on the backseat. On the other side of the windshield, a long line of cars stretches to a place my father calls infinity. I move my lips, and I pray, "Please, God, make them move."

My father shakes his head. His fingers tap the wheel. I hold my breath, making myself small and still. If I'm very quiet, maybe my father won't yank the wheel, pull out into the empty lane beside us, and drive home. He does that, changes direction without warning. Then, I see it, a horse racing across a field, the rider bent low. In trouble.

Summers, when my father was a boy, he worked at the pony ride on the Boardwalk, holding the reins and leading children around the ring. When I was a baby, he lifted me up into a saddle, then led me around the same track. I have pictures of me when I'm one, sitting on a pony's back, my father's hand steadying me. When I'm three, I ride alone. My father slaps the pony into a trot. The pony canters. I hold his mane in my fists. Still, I fall off, fall down into the grit, hitting my hip, scraping skin. Blood seeps, then flows. I let out a long, deep howl. My father ties his handkerchief around my knee, lifts me up, sits me down into the saddle. "You don't want to be a crybaby, do you?"

I want to be brave like my father, so when he takes off across an empty field that morning in July and chases a runaway horse, I'm not surprised, I'm furious. I belong in that field, running beside my father. The rider is a girl. I see her long hair, streaming. Then, I see the shape of her sliding down, riding along the horse's flank. I climb up into the front seat, lean over my mother's lap, and stretch my body outside the opened window. The chrome burns. I don't care. I am calling to my father.

That afternoon, telling the story to Grandma Rose, my father boasts, "She coulda been killed. Lucky for her I was there. No telling what woulda happened. I headed him off, then grabbed the reins. You shoulda seen her face. She couldn't thank me enough. Couldn't thank me enough." We're sitting on a rough, wool blanket on the sand, my mother, my father, and me. Grandma Rose sits in her beach chair. My grandpa Harry, who isn't my real grandfather, just a man married to Rose, isn't with us. Sandal, my real grandfather, died when my father was twelve, and this, I learn early, is the great sadness of my father's life and the reason I must be nice to my father. At all times.

Grandma Rose reaches for her bathing cap. She takes my hand. This isn't the first time my father has told that story. "Come," Rose says to me.

My father's smile twists. The corners of his mouth turn down. Overhead gulls wheel. "Where're you taking her?" he asks Rose.

"For a swim," Rose says.

"She just ate," my father says.

"We'll dip our toes," Rose says.

Now, my father's story is gone, swallowed up by something I can't name. I stand at the edge of the blanket, looking down at the sand, tiny grains of tan and white, flecked with brown, flecked with sparkles, sinking down under my feet as I walk, stretching my legs, then leaping, matching Rose's stride. Rose smiles. "A regular gazelle," she says to me.

Gazelle is a funny word, and I laugh. Rose laughs, too. Secretly (secretly, because I can't tell my father, although I'm not sure why), I look up to Rose. She's pretty, and she's fun. She's like my father. Like me. We have a certain sparkle in our eyes, a zest when we walk. We're strong-minded and strong-willed. We're volatile, the kind of people who act before we think. Not that I can say these things about us, not then. I know them, though, know, too, what my father is doing this very minute, sitting on our blanket, smoking a Lucky Strike, fuming, and complaining to my mother. About me. About Rose.

Today, Rose's suit is turquoise blue. It has a deep V that shows the cleft in her breasts. It has legs. She doesn't wear those old-lady skirts. Her skin is tanned, all these summers in Asbury Park, winters in Miami Beach. She smells sweet, like coconut candy. The ocean licks my toes, rises to my knees. I look back. On the beach, blankets blend into sand; figures watch without faces. A wave rolls. "Jump," Rose says.

Together, we fly up and over the wave's curl.

That night, my father slaps a dime on the number seven. The Boardwalk is crowded, rides and concessions. The air smells of salt and sea, sugar and hot oil. People push. My father lifts me up and sets me down on the edge of the counter. The wheel of fortune spins. Spins and spins. Rose leans and whispers. "You're going to win."

"Number seven," the barker shouts. "Number seven, the winner here. Give the little lady choice of the stand."

2.

I am eleven when Sarah, my other grandmother, dies. Sarah isn't Rose. I don't want to *be* Sarah, but I love her with all of the love I hold tight inside of me. My mother covers the mirrors. She pushes the furniture to the walls. My uncles bring wooden crates for us to sit on. This is called sitting *shiva*. My father, a Reform Jew, a modern Jew, doesn't believe in sitting *shiva*. He beckons, and I follow. I climb into his yellow Studebaker and slam the door. "Where're we going?"

"The relatives are coming from New York."

I nod and pretend I understand. We drive and park in front of the new deli. Inside, my father buys salami and rolled beef. Where does he think he's taking that meat? "Dad," I say.

"What?" he says, silencing me.

In the kitchen, I curve my back and lean into the doorframe, feeling the wood with the bumps of my spine. A swinging door leads to the dining room, and I am poised to escape. All of my aunts and uncles have gathered here to watch my father roll and place each slice of meat on a platter, a *flesig* platter that has never held un*kosher* meat, and that's what I say, hardly realizing I'm speaking out loud. "It's not *kosher*."

A piercing quiet holds my words, holds them like the aftermath of a siren's wail. My father's eyes find my face, and he glares.

"What's not *kosher*?" Uncle Gabe's voice booms. Gabe is Sarah's favorite son. The feisty one.

I don't answer.

"The meat, right?" Uncle Gabe says. "Your father brought *traif* into the house."

I look down. I'm wearing saddle shoes that I've polished myself. The white streaks. I can never polish smoothly, never keep the white from edging up over the brown. My laces are dirty. Inside the plaid, the white has grayed.

"Take it out," Gabe says to my father. He is not a tall man, but he is solid.

"You're telling *me* what to do," my father says.

"It's a house of mourning," Gabe says.

"They're coming from New York. What do you want them to eat?"

"Please," my aunt Betty says.

"You stay out of this," my father says.

"You don't talk to my wife that way," Gabe says.

"What? What did I say?"

Uncle Gabe reaches for the platter. "If you don't take it out, I will."

"Over my dead body."

The platter totters. My mother catches it. My father is pushing, pushing and pointing into Uncle Gabe's chest, tapping with his index finger. My uncle heaves him back. My father's shoulder hits the refrigerator. He recovers, quickly, swings a punch, and misses. Uncle Gabe lifts a hand. A gesture of surrender. "Enough already."

My father doesn't answer. He lands a blow to the side of my uncle's head. Gabe's glasses fly and crash. My uncle Irving picks up the broken frame. He curses my father. *A fayer zol du trefin,* you should burn up. *Di beyner zol du oysrinen,* may your bones be drained of marrow. *Du zol vaksn vi a tsibele mit dem kop in drerd,* you should grow like an onion with its head in the ground.

Uncle Gabe lands a blow on my father's chin. A tiny cut opens. My mother shrieks. Uncle Irving pushes my father. Uncle Harry pushes Gabe. Separated, the two men glare. They blow out their breath. I slink back and wiggle through the tiny opening between the swinging door and the frame. Noiselessly, I climb the stairs. Outside, car doors slam. Engines start. The house is still, the air hanging so quietly, I realize I'm holding my breath, listening for a single sound, one that will tell me where my father is. I want to hear the engine of the Studebaker starting up, then revving. That will mean Father has left. Stormed out. Instead, I hear footsteps in the dining room, then on the stairs. A heavy silence crushes my heart. I feel him. I hear his breathing. He has to knock. *In this house we knock. We don't just open a door.* My door flies open. My father glares; my father shouts. "See what you did. See what trouble you caused. Now are you happy?" He yanks my arm, then lets go. I fall off my bed, scramble up, grab a pillow, and hold on.

"I'm talking to you."

Silence.

"I said I'm talking to you. Now answer me."

"What? What did I do?"

He mocks me. "What? What did I do?"

"Stop it."

"Stop it."

"I hate you. Hate your guts."

My father's eyes turn to glass. He unbuckles his belt, pulls it, slowly, through the loops. I can't believe what I'm seeing. My father is not swinging his belt, bringing it down on my shoulders, my arm, my leg. I scramble from my bed. I cower in a corner. I cry; I beg. "Please, Daddy, please. No more. I'll be good. I promise."

But my father has a rhythm now, some terrible force driving him from the inside out. He brings the belt down on my flesh, each stroke a word he spits from his tongue. "Show you. Own damn fault. Can't keep your mouth shut. Can you? Can you?"

Time turns to burning flesh, and I feel as if I'm dying here under my father's belt.

Now, my mother's figure fills the doorway. Where was she? Where was my damn mother? She whispers my father's name. "Leo. Leo."

My father snaps his head. "You stay out of this."

I think she's announcing an arrival—the relatives from New York, my aunt Ida, my uncle Nat, my cousins, Seymour and Lorraine.

"Leo," she says, "Rose is here. Your mother."

And in my mother's voice, I hear not reproof, but warning.

Rose calls up the stairs. "Leo, where is everybody? What're you doing? What's going on?"

My father slips the tongue of his belt through the loops. "Don't think I'm finished with you," he says to me.

But he is. And I know it.

3.

I am a precocious, ponytailed, cinch-waisted teenager. I go to dances; I date boys, boys who drive cars. I come home with my lipstick smeared and my cheeks on fire. My father flicks the porch light, blinking it on and off. "Gotta go," I mutter to Danny. He holds on, lips groping for my lips, fingers searching under my bra.

I push him away, then reach for the door handle. Our house sits on a rise. Neighbors have planted rock gardens on the slope. We have grass my father can't mow. Danny lags behind on the steep wooden steps. The front door opens. Danny stops. I want to turn back and flee with him to his car. My feet won't move.

"You're late," my father yells. "I thought I told you eleven o'clock."

After the movie, Danny and I drove a winding road to the top of South Mountain, watched the lights of New York City across the river, dreamed our dreams, kissed and kissed. Now, I watch my father's waist. If he moves right, I'll move left, slip past him, race up the stairs, and into my room. I'll grab a chair, then shove the back of it under the knob. No locks, not on the bedroom doors. Locks on the bathroom doors, but I'm not allowed to use them. *What if something happens? How can we save you?*

Inside the small hallway, my father presses his fingers into my arm. My flesh turns white. He shouts, and he spits. His face contorts. "Do you know what time it is? Where have you been? Look at you. You should see yourself."

Danny's car starts up. The motor sounds, then fades. I stiffen under my father's touch. "Let go. If you don't let go, I'll call up Grandma Rose. I'll tell her you're beating me."

His grip loosens, and he mumbles. "Bitch."

I don't care what he calls me. I'm gone, flying up the stairs and into my room. Now my father's fury pounds the door. Let him shout. He won't come in, I know he won't.

"I'm warning you, Shelly, keep this up, and you're out on the street. You think I don't mean it? You're no good, do you hear? No damn good."

I lie on my bed fully dressed, bladder full, afraid to leave my room and use the toilet. My belly aches. Urine leaks. I feel it inside my underpants. I think of Danny's hand sliding under my blouse, under my bra, and I feel ashamed. I hold tight between my legs. Maybe I am what my father says I am, a tramp, a slut, a lousy whore.

4.

My father calls from his store. This is what my father does. Owns a camera store. He and my mother work together. My mother sells film and greeting cards. My father sells cameras and enlargers. "I'm bringing your grandmother home," he says to me. "I want you to stay with her until I can bring her back."

Rose no longer spends her summers in Asbury Park or her winters in Miami Beach. Harry died years before. Rose lives in a house that is part rooming house, part nursing home, along with three other old people. She is not allowed to leave. I wonder how Rose got to my father's store. "I took the bus," Rose tells me.

"Three buses," my father says, shaking his head. He looks at me. "You'll be all right? You won't let her leave?"

We're standing in the driveway, Rose, my father, and I. I'm nineteen, a sophomore in college, home on spring break. I reassure my father, then take Rose's arm. Her skin is so soft I feel her bones. Inside the house, she steps back. "Let me look at you." Her eyes are gentle, like fingers on my skin. She smiles. Her blue eyes glint. "A real looker. Like me. I'm still not bad, am I?" She turns for me to see.

That afternoon Rose and I play double solitaire. We play gin. Rose wins six games out of ten. We watch game shows on TV. We pop popcorn, then toss kernels into the air and try to catch them in our mouths. At five-thirty, my mother arrives. I lift a brown paper shopping bag from her arms. Inside are veal chops, a head of iceberg lettuce she'll cut into wedges. I stir Hellmann's mayonnaise and Heinz ketchup, making Russian dressing. Rose sits at the kitchen table. She opens the bakery box my mother carried home and peers inside. She sticks a finger in the frosting, then licks. "Whipped cream. Why isn't this in the icebox?"

After supper, my father tells Rose he's taking her home. Rose says her room is cold. When Rose complains, Mrs. Ledger, the landlady, tells her to shut up. "Imagine that," Rose says. And that isn't all. Mrs. Ledger can't cook. Nothing has any taste. Rose has not left the kitchen table. She sits in her chair as if she's claimed it. "This is the first decent meal I've eaten in God knows when."

Tears cloud Rose's blue eyes. They fall down onto her cheeks. Standing behind Rose's chair, I grip her shoulders. My father mouths a single word. "Senile."

Yeah, right, I want to say. Instead, I kiss Rose's hair. She cries, softly.

My father rubs his bald head with two fingers. It is a gesture of frustration. He is tired. Wearing down. "Let's go," he says to Rose.

I watch my father carefully. Will he blow or give in? I take the risk. "She can sleep with me. I'll drive you to work, then take her back in the morning."

My father doesn't speak.

"It's not a bad idea," my mother says. She scrubs the broiler pan.

My father drifts toward the living room. He turns on the TV. Soon, all of us sit and watch.

This is the one and only year Ford has made a hardtop convertible, a Skyliner, and my father owns one. I drop him at the store, drive out of town, then pull to the side of the road. I push a button to lower the top. This is risky. Sometimes, the damn thing sticks halfway, then you have to drive to a service station with the roof of the car arcing like an umbrella. Today, it slips back easily. I hand Rose a kerchief. She ties it around her hair. I tie one around my hair. I turn on the radio, The Platters, Elvis Presley, then music from *Gigi*, "Thank Heaven for Little Girls." Rose sings along, as we fly down the Garden State.

At the Shore, mostly, the concessions are boarded up. Still, Rose and I walk the Boardwalk. "Remember the day your father won that teddy bear?" she says to me. "It was bigger than you were."

"Lucky seven."

"That's it," Rose says.

I spot an open hot dog stand where I order two hot dogs, two root beers, and fries that come inside paper cone cups. The day is sunny, but windy. I've brought along sweaters and coats. Rose and I sit on a bench facing the sea. The beach stretches in front of us. There are no blankets, no umbrellas, just sand and the ever-present, ever-rolling sea. Rose bites her hot dog. She chews. "You're a good girl," she says to me. "You're smart, and you're lucky. You'll finish college. You'll be somebody. Don't let anybody stop you. Are you listening to me?"

"I'm listening."

5.

Rose is the youngest of six siblings, all boys, the only child living at home when Simon, her father, dies. Like my father, Rose is a child of early loss. Hannah, Rose's mother, runs a boarding house. The family is poor. Rose leaves school and goes to work. She is young. She is beautiful. I imagine her wearing a tailored shirtwaist with leg-of-mutton sleeves, a high collar, an ascot tied at her neck. Her dark floor-length skirt falls from her tiny waist. She reaches back to close the outside door, then steps down onto the sidewalk. She walks to the corner where she boards a trolley, riding out of her lower-class Jewish neighborhood and into Center City, where she works at Wanamaker's modeling gloves. She meets men.

Rose visits Albert, her brother who lives in New York City. Albert moves from job to job. He calls himself an inventor. He makes rich friends. One of those friends is Sandal Green. Before Albert introduces Sandal to Rose, he wags a finger in his sister's face. "I'm warning you, Rosie, don't fool around with this one."

Rose is twenty-eight and pregnant when she marries Sandal. Sandal's family sends him to dental school. My uncle is born in Maryland. When Sandal finishes school, his father buys him a house in New Jersey. A river and a world separate Rose and Sandal from Sandal's family in Manhattan. Eight years pass before my father is born. When my father is twelve, Sandal rolls off a couch and dies at his feet. My father skips school. He sits on a park bench, staring into space. Rose takes in boarders. Sandal has left her not only with unfathomable grief, but with a ledger of unpaid accounts and a mortgage to pay.

6.

I wake in my virginal bed, my husband's erection prodding my ass, his arm flung over my body. My bedroom door is closed. "No," I say to my husband.

"Why not?"

I feel my father in these walls, see his eyes on the ceiling. I fling back the covers. In the bathroom, I shower and wash my hair. Dressed in jeans and a man's shirt, I walk down the stairs. In spite of the fact that this is the first time in the ten days we have been married that I cannot make love with my husband, I feel a certain freedom. Or is it smugness? I'm a married woman. I've had sex, and my father can't get me. "Good morning," I chirp.

My father sits at the kitchen table. He doesn't speak, nor does he lift his eyes to look at me. He picks up his cup of coffee, and he slurps.

"Good morning," my mother says. "Sleep well?"

I assume she heard me in the bathroom, then on the stairs, because now she's scrambling eggs, anticipating in the way she does. She scoops eggs onto a plate. My father stands. He lifts the newspaper from the table. My husband enters. My father mumbles and leaves the kitchen. Did he say good morning? Now, my mother is scrambling two more eggs, asking my husband how he likes them.

"Soft," my husband says.

"Soft," my mother says.

In this house we like our eggs cooked hard and well.

"Like this?" my mother says.

"Perfect," my husband says.

After breakfast, my mother and I fall into a rhythm. I carry dishes to the sink. She rinses and loads the dishwasher. I tell her about Bermuda, the lush flowers, the turquoise sea, the motorbikes we rented and drove all over the island.

My mother nods. She is happy for me.

The next day, my husband and I board a plane for Cincinnati, my new home. On the plane my husband pulls two folded pieces of paper from his shirt pocket. One is clearly a bill, the other in my father's handwriting turns out to be an invoice, too. "I guess these came in while we were away."

The first is from my dentist. A bride needs bright teeth. The second in my father's scrawl is for twenty dollars, numbers and letters. Shoes. One pair.

"So?" I say.

"So, he figures they're mine."

My father gave me a budget for my trousseau. Five hundred dollars. I went over. One bright set of teeth. One pair of shoes from Beck's.

My husband laughs.

I look out the plane's window feeling myself grow smaller. It's a familiar feeling, this shrinking into nothingness.

My husband touches my shoulder. He leans, and he whispers. "Hey. It's nothing. Really. I don't mind."

One final lashing. I stuff the bills into my purse. "I'm writing the check." That's the way it is. I have money of my own. Not much, but it's mine. I have a job I'm heading to.

"Okay."

"I mean it."

"I said okay."

7.

I am beginning my sixth month of pregnancy when my father calls to tell me Rose has died in her sleep. "A blessing," my father says.

I'm not yet old enough to consider death a blessing, and as the family gathers in a tiny parlor inside this funeral home, I'm feeling bereft. I'd wanted so much to introduce this new life I'm carrying to Grandma Rose. In the chapel a young rabbi who has never met Rose describes her as a loving wife, a loving mother, a loving grandmother. He looks at my cousins; he looks at me. Tears stream down my cheeks. I'm trying to cry silently, but a sob escapes. I see Rose in my mind's eye. She is dancing at my wedding the year before, wearing a blue dress, always blue to match her eyes, joining a circle on the dance floor, lifting her arms and dancing a *hora*. I broke the circle to dance with Rose.

Inside me, this baby kicks. I've felt movement before, that watery turning, but this is the first swift kick, a kick so hard it seems to lodge under my ribs. It has lodged under my ribs. A knee? A foot? I can't breathe, nor can I sit inside this stifling chapel, listening to the rabbi's lies. *He* didn't know Rose. *He* didn't love Rose. My husband's fingers find my hand. "Are you all right?"

"I need air."

"I'll come."

I shake my head. "Stay."

He gives me that look, as if to say, What do you really want?

On the sidewalk, I fold my arms over the lump of baby inside of me. It is June. The air smells sweet. Honeysuckle. The first roses.

Later, when the hearse pulls away from the curb, my uncle, my aunt, and my cousins follow in my uncle's Buick, next is my father driving his white four-seater T-Bird, my mother sitting upright beside him. My husband and I do not join the procession. Philadelphia is a two-hour drive. I've traveled enough. Grieved enough.

More than twenty-five years pass before I visit Rose's grave. My son, the child born just three months after Rose's death, takes me there. He lives in Philadelphia, and I can't get past the irony of this young man, raised in Massachusetts, then New Hampshire, choosing a graduate school in Philadelphia, where he walks the same sidewalks Rose walked. He knows how to reach Adath Jeshurun, the cemetery where Rose is buried. We ride the subway, and when it surfaces, I look out at the shells of buildings gutted by fires, their windows empty and boarded up. Remnants of past riots. Are they left like that purposely? Or because they can be?

We leave the platform and walk through an inner city neighborhood. Years before this was a Jewish neighborhood. In a way, it still is. Jews are buried here, and the upkeep of the cemetery is guaranteed. Perpetual care. The grass is mowed and trimmed back from the paths. A large headstone marks the family plot. They're all here, Simon and Hannah, Rose and Sandal. I sit and weigh stones in my palm, feeling the heft of them. Now, I place a pebble on Rose's headstone. I add another and another. I am balancing; I am building. A tower of remembrance. For Rose.

8.

My mother is ill. The doctors called her attacks TIAs, Transient Ischemic Attacks, transient because a clot that lodges in an artery in her brain, time after time, causing her to lose use of her left leg, her left arm and hand, to lose her speech, passes through. Transient, but not benign. She walks with a limp and a cane. Her speech is impaired. She and my father, having joined that great migration from north to south, live in Florida, one of those places that offers independent living, then assisted living, and finally nursing care.

In the apartment, I help my mother undress. We have come upstairs after dinner, and she is tired, so tired. My father is downstairs, chairing a meeting. He is on the board here, and I'm reminded of my childhood, all of those rushed suppers, my father leaving, going to his bowling league, his meetings, Boy Scout Commissioners, Kiwanis, Chamber of Commerce. I slip a blouse from my mother's shoulders, then lift her skirt over her head. I take her bra and her panties. Naked, my mother looks shrunken, lost inside her own skin, all of that loose flesh, bruises where needles entered her veins, more bruises on her legs. She no longer heals. It's those blood-thinning drugs. So many drugs, so many illnesses. I hold her nightgown, then slide it over her frail body. She climbs up into bed. I perch beside her. Alone, we tell stories. My mother begins. "You know about Bob the butcher, don't you?"

This is a story shrouded in whispers, hidden inside the old language, *di shande,* a shame, *shh, dos kind,* shh, the child.

"Your father was a teenager. Bob was Rose's boyfriend. He was a butcher. Maybe he lived in the neighborhood, I don't know. He wasn't Jewish. He used to help her out. In those days, you shoveled coal. It was hard work. She was a widow, a woman alone. I guess she was lonely. Bob moved in. He lived there maybe three years."

"Lived there. You mean?"

My mother nods. "Can you imagine what that did to your father?"

I burst out laughing.

"What's funny? It's not funny."

I close my mouth and will myself to stop smiling. I want this story. If I laugh, I won't get it.

"Your father told her. He said if she married Bob, he'd run away. He'd live on the streets. He'd starve, he'd beg. He didn't care what happened to him. Now, isn't that an awful thing?"

So this is the great secret of my father's life. It wasn't Sandal's death that made my father into the man he is and was. It was Rose and her lover. How old was he then, sixteen? And filled to bursting with rage. And shame. I see my father. I see Rose. I see a cinch-waisted, ponytailed girl, racing up a flight of stairs. I see a child, looking up the length of her father's trouser leg. "Me, too. Me, too."

I know why my mother is telling my father's secret. She wants "to make peace." That's her job, always has been. *Stop it, both of you. Leo, say you're sorry. Shelly, apologize.* Yet, these days, my father and I hardly fight. We back off. But, my mother is wise. She fears space, that large gulf between my father and me. What will happen if she dies? Who will send my father cards on Father's Day, on his birthday? Who will visit? So she asks for my sympathy and my understanding. Not in words, our family doesn't work that way. We tell stories. And this is what we have, what we all have, fictions to carry our truths.

"If it wasn't for Rose and Bob, your father would've finished college. He would've become a dentist like his father. Rose failed him."

I get the message. Don't you fail him, too.

A key in the lock. My father's footsteps in the hall, his frame filling the doorway. He is still a large man. "I'm telling you, if it wasn't for me, we never would've gotten it through. They didn't want to do it. Didn't want to upset management. I said to them, 'We're a board. That's what we're for. If we don't upset management, who will?'" He glances at my mother. "You want anything? A dish of ice cream?"

She shakes her head. "You?" my mother says to me.

"No thanks."

"Chocolate. It's good," my father says. "Have some."

"Maybe later."

"Later's too late."

9.

I walk the white X painted onto the dark macadam, heel to toe, measuring. It's quiet here this Sunday morning. No swish of cars. No rumble of trucks. No warning from a train's whistle. I'm sure, though, my father didn't skid, didn't try to step on the brake. If he had, he would've gone sideways into the tall, tall grass and then the post where a black lettered sign announces the crossing. The sign is round, the background painted a bright yellow, black block letters filling the angles of an X—RAILROAD.

The land here is thick with undergrowth, scrub bushes, palmetto, coconut palms with their skinny, curving trunks, their mop heads of fronds. There are pines, evergreens, although I know they, too, lose their needles, and I'm reminded that nothing is forever, not even old, old age. In the two years since my mother's death, I have been a dutiful, if somewhat distant daughter. I'd like to say my father and I learned to speak our minds, and in that way we reached peace. What we reached was a truce, a line drawn, protected by mined fields where we didn't walk. I visited twice a year. I sent gifts. My father, too, sent gifts. To me. To my sons. And that's what he was doing that day, driving out to a grove, buying oranges to ship north.

I run my palm over the feathery tops of tall grasses, pulling a stalk, then chewing the sweet tender end, pacing, now the distance from signpost to tracks. There is no gate, but the warnings are clear, the sign itself in the shape of a pinwheel, letters written on the crossbucks. The lights are dark, the color of port wine or old Chianti. I imagine them lighted and flashing, imagine my father's foot bearing down hard on accelerator, trying to beat the train. He liked speed, that revved-up feeling, and I'm reminded of a runaway horse all those years ago and of my father racing across a field of grass, reminded, too, of my own brushes with danger, the trees I climbed and fell out of, the mountain I skied in the Alps, losing my way, finally emerging after dark. That's what that feeling did, it made you a hero; it made you dead.

I look for clues, the mark of a tire, a piece of rubber blown out. The crossing itself is rough and uneven. I pick up a piece of glass. Not glass. Too thin. Easily flaked. Nothing but mica. I toss it away. Whatever was left of my father's car has either been carted away or ground down into the grit under my feet. What are the chances of car and train meeting like that? Of life and death held in the balance of seconds or less? Win or lose. One more dime on the number seven, slapped down on the wheel of fortune that Rose, my father, and I played, the three of us watching a metal tooth hit spokes, slow down, jump, and click, before it settled on a tiny black diamond in the center, the exact center, where it trembled, threatening to click into the red and onto number eight. Holding our breath, we watched it shiver, willing the barker to call out, "Number seven. Number seven, the winner here. Give the little lady choice of the stand."

I walk along beside the tracks, a single pair of them riding a stone railroad bed, coming together, then disappearing. It is as if the glinting steel has reached an end, as if a train traveling on this track will suddenly find itself out of rails, but the rails continue, I know that. The engineer knew. I imagine him blowing a whistle, pulling down on the chain of the brake, bringing an entire freight train to a screeching halt, but not before hitting my father's car. Instantly. It's what I've been told. What I choose to believe.

I drive east toward the sea, a cardboard box covered with blue velvet sits beside me in the passenger's seat. "Why buy an urn when you're going to scatter the ashes anyway?" the funeral director said. He spoke the same words when my mother died. She is here, too. There is no Boardwalk, no pony track, no wheel of fortune. There are palm trees. There are benches. There is sand where I imagine Grandma Rose sitting in her metal beach chair, resting her elbows on the arms. She is the Rose I remember, wearing a one-piece turquoise suit, a wide-brimmed straw hat, cocked jauntily to one side. I nod to her ghost as I carry my father toward the sea.

ABOUT CORNELIUS EADY

A Profile by Natasha Trethewey

Cornelius Eady spent his entire childhood in Rochester, New York, a destination for many African Americans during the early twentieth-century migration. Though Rochester had once been a frontier town known for its radicalism and such famous residents as Susan B. Anthony and Frederick Douglass, by the time Eady was born there in 1954, it had become somewhat provincial, a conservative place good for raising kids, which suited Eady's parents just fine. They had moved to the city from Florida because of the promise of union jobs and the opportunity to buy property, and their house was comfortably situated in a tight-knit African-American community, on a dead-end street, in a neighborhood once populated by Italians.

The Eadys' backyard, filled with apricot trees and grape arbors, with its close proximity to the Pennsylvania Railroad, gave a precocious, would-be poet plenty to explore, plenty of images to store away as future material. Still, he had a longing for more than his hometown had to offer, and for a while his restlessness was satisfied by books. When Eady wasn't investigating the bounty of things right in his own backyard, he was entrenched at the Rundell Public Library, reading everything he could get his hands on, including the works of poets like William Carlos Williams, Amiri Baraka, Pablo Neruda, and Allen Ginsberg. Since his family was too poor at the time to buy a record player or albums, Eady also spent hours at the library listening to records, sampling everything the library had, fostering his eclectic tastes in music. He loved what he heard there, and in the music of his parents' voices at home. In their speech he encountered the cadences they'd brought North with them, as well as a language rich in metaphor, and he began to do the kind of listening necessary to become a poet—a poet with a finely tuned ear and skillfully rendered musicality in his verse.

Writing poetry, however, was not what Eady's father thought of then as a practical thing to do; figuring out how to make a living was. Yet Eady's seventh-grade homeroom teacher, Joanna Mason, noticed his talent for rhyme and lyrical expression right away, as did others in the school. One of his first efforts was a poem about the assassination of Martin Luther King, Jr., and Eady vividly recalls its reception: "People were coming up to me, telling me how they had been thinking exactly what I'd articulated for them in the poem. I realized then poetry's larger implications." With his teacher's encouragement, Eady eventually transferred to Rochester Educational Alternative for his junior and senior years—a free school modeled after the Summerhill method that he remembers as the "hippest place in Rochester." He spent almost all his time there, engaged in "marathon writing sessions." He'd write poems for days straight, and in the evenings would sleep over at the homes of friends, in one of which he met Sarah Micklem, the woman he would marry.

After high school, Eady stayed in Rochester to attend Empire State University, where he discovered he could major in English with a concentration in creative writing. It was during this time that he began searching for collections of poems in which he might see himself reflected, works by black poets that might provide a kind of validation. Among others, he ran across a collection of poems by Yusef Komunyakaa. "I was thrilled," Eady says, "because it was that moment when you actually find yourself in the books you're reading."

From that point on, Eady embarked on the creation of his own body of work. To date, he has published seven collections of poetry: *Kartunes* (1980); *Victims of the Latest Dance Craze* (1985), which won the Lamont Poetry Prize from the Academy of American Poets; *BOOM BOOM BOOM* (1988); *The Gathering of My Name* (1991); *You Don't Miss Your Water* (1995); *The Autobiography of a Jukebox* (1997); and *Brutal Imagination* (2001), which was a finalist for the National Book Award. He has been the recipient of numerous honors, including grants and fellowships from the National Endowment for the Arts, the Guggenheim Foundation, the Rockefeller Foundation, and the Lila Wallace–Reader's Digest Fund. He was an associate professor at the State University of New York at Stony Brook, where he also served as Director of the Poetry Center, and is currently Visiting Writer at the City College of New York. He lives in Manhattan with his wife of twenty-three

Miriam Berkley

years, Sarah Micklem, and has been busy of late with theater pro-
ductions. A cycle of poems from his most recent book was the
basis for a libretto for a roots opera, *Running Man,* on which he
collaborated with Diedre Murray, and which was a finalist for the
1999 Pulitzer Prize. And the main sequence from *Brutal Imagination* was adapted into a play that opened off-Broadway last fall at
The Vineyard.

Yet, even with his personal success, Eady never forgot the lack of
community he had felt as a young poet, and thought he could and
should do something more. In 1996, Eady and the poet Toi Derricotte founded Cave Canem. "It began as a series of conversations
with various black writers and scholars," he says, "loose talk that
often ended when the question of money arose. Then Sarah, my
wife, suggested we just pay for it ourselves. For the first two years,
we did." Since then, the Cave Canem retreat, a summer workshop
for African-American poets, has flourished, inviting approximate-
ly fifty-two new and returning fellows each year to work on their
craft. In addition, they've established an annual book prize that includes publication by presses such as Graywolf and the University
of Georgia, and overall have created a community that celebrates
the diversity and richness of African-American literature. Indeed,

one of Cave Canem's main achievements has been its declaration of another tradition in American poetry, one that is no monolith, but that is varied and important. Note Eady's unflinching lines from the poem "Gratitude":

> I have survived
> > Long enough
> > To tell a bit
>
> Of an old story.
> > And to those
> > > who defend poetry
> > > against all foreign tongues:
>
> Love.
> > And to those who believe
> > > a dropped clause
> > > signifies encroachment:
>
> Love.
> > And to the bullies who need
> > > the musty air of
> > > the clubhouse
>
> All to themselves:
> > I am a brick in a house
> > > that is being built
> > > around your house.

Whereas many poets shy away from a political agenda, Eady is clearly unafraid to embrace one. "I tell my students that it is a thing to face if you are a black poet. People will say your writing is political and that you are writing about race even when you think you're not, even when you think you're just writing about the people you know best."

After the publication of his most recent collection, *Brutal Imagination*, his niece remarked, "Good, you've started writing political stuff again." The title sequence of the book presents visions of the black man in the white imagination. Eady assumes the voices of several African Americans from popular culture—Uncle Tom, Uncle Ben, Steppin Fetchit—but for the most part, he draws upon the infamous case of Susan Smith in Union, South Carolina, writing from the point of view of the imaginary black man she had invented as an alibi for her murder of her two sons. In *Brutal Imagination,* Eady gets to the heart of a frightening and sad state of affairs—that the image of the black man in America is such that a story like Smith's could be readily believed. Mr. Zero, as Eady calls the imaginary carjacker, becomes a mirror for all of us, a way to contemplate how far we have and have not come. In an earlier poem, "Anger," Eady wrote: "It would be difficult to stuff my anger into an envelope." What is beautiful about Eady's work is the way in which the poems themselves become envelopes, containers for the elegant missives of his characters' voices—not angry in their tone, but piercing, quiet, intelligent—reflections of Cornelius Eady's wonderfully restless spirit.

Natasha Trethewey's second collection of poems, Bellocq's Ophelia, *has just been released by Graywolf Press, which also published her first book,* Domestic Work. *She teaches at Emory University.*

OUBLIETTE *Poems by Peter Richards. Verse Press, $12.00 paper. Reviewed by David Rivard.*

If you are a poet of any seriousness, you make a style for your-self out of one essential contradiction: the "thinginess" of experi-ence, of thinking and feeling, and especially of silence, can't be captured by words. The most distinctive stylists of the generation of poets now in their twenties and thirties are compelling because they already understand this. They include, to name a few, Olena Kalytiak Davis, Joshua Beckman, Cate Marvin, Joe Wenderoth, Liz Powell, Joseph Lease, and Josh Weiner. Of this handful, none seems more original than Peter Richards. He is certainly the most visionary, if by visionary you mean subversive and extrasensory.

Richards's way of dealing with this contradiction is to turn it inside out. He lets language feed off its own juices, improvising out of music and association. The obvious influences on *Oubliette,* his first book, are Stevens, Ashbery, and Merwin; but, in spirit at least, the erotic playfulness in the book is closer to that of a poet like Yehuda Amichai. For Richards, life in a poem is like life in a body—most at risk, and most fully itself, when at play.

Richards likes to put a singular physical sensation at the center of a poem, a sensation that acts as a magnet for forces felt all over the body. In "The Drawstring Hisses," the title itself is a sound flung like a line into some interior pond. It dredges up other sounds, all of them teeming with creaturely existence. At heart, Richards is an ecstatic: "could one intonate the gown of passing near / from the gown of passing by / my own gown would cast this cast-out ragged hue / clear beyond concession or settle for the sounds / I hear the soprano half of my insolence / request from the nudes / fanning out to a shrill / gossamer shrill...."

The purpose of all this invention seems to be an education in happenstance. As if any human life—all its possibilities and tragedies—might be made simply out of accident. "With this one kiss I now accept the modern city. / ... I accept catalogs for holiday candy need to be clearly conceived, / and bins for commingled containers color-coded for days" ("Central Square"). But to be open to possibility and play is to be open to mistake and illusion, too. The dislocations can be disturbing: "From the window with deep spoons a street lamp offers your breast. / Tonight will I take you without seeing your breast? / Spine like a staircase, leave me astray."

In Peter Richards's poems a terrible loneliness lurks around the edges of happenstance. It's a metaphysical loneliness, and nothing—not even the immortality of a god—can offer protection from it: "In that, I sometimes fear I am deathless—fear for now on I'll serve as the points / upon which various and misguided winds / can agree. They agree I'm afraid / and that fears will keep them safe" ("Remainder").

These various and misguided forces are demonic. Underneath the surfaces of everyday life, there are "elemental powers turning somersaults," as Czeslaw Milosz says, "and devils, mocking the naïve who believe in them." In "A Third Tree," Richards echoes this: "O we had sunrises / and such natural effects as a cowbell and wood violets / comprising the quiet. Where it put love to sleep I saw no good / reason proceeding and the death mask gardens can be."

The place where erotic playfulness and metaphysical terror touch in these poems is in their syntax. Unlike most poets of his generation who use fugal structures, Richards is interested in locating the action of thinking and feeling in the flux of line-to-line movement. Most poets are stiffs in comparison. For Richards, it's not so much that syntax focuses language as that it focuses the reader. Along with his cat's paw sense of diction, it allows him to brew up a tonal soup that is one part tenderness, one part comic slyness, and one part awe. And it suggests that his range as a poet will be wide and continually surprising.

David Rivard's most recent book is Bewitched Playground *(Graywolf). He is a Guggenheim fellow for 2001, and he teaches at Tufts University.*

WAVEMAKER II *A novel by Mary-Beth Hughes. Grove/Atlantic Monthly, $24.00 cloth. Reviewed by Fred Leebron.*

In her admirable debut novel, *Wavemaker II,* Mary-Beth Hughes stitches together a complex story of an unraveling family against the backdrop of the early 1960's misdoings of Roy Cohn, the controversial McCarthy-era lawyer. While the storyline is full of daring shifts in point of view and authentic historical details, what holds the work together is the essential authority and music of the narrative voice.

Hughes successfully evokes the nearly catastrophic summer of 1964, when Will Clemens, who has loyally taken the fall for Roy Cohn in a sketchy situation, endures his prison term while his young family fractures. Kay, his wife, finds herself susceptible to virtually every seduction, as she faces her young son's battle with terminal cancer and her mildly obese daughter's maddeningly inappropriate forays into the sex-charged world of adolescence. As Will suffers through a variety of humiliations and finds himself growing more and more immoral, Kay accepts into her bed men whom she would never have once considered, and her boy, Bo, slips further and further into the oblivion of his illness.

It's a grim and yet lyrically vivid period in this young family's life, when nothing is going right, when the world is in league against them, and Hughes captures this with a wondrous array of sensual detail and a keen eye for the telling gesture and the crystallized perception. Will's soap, to Kay's senses, has "a kind of scent like shoe polish in a tin." The prison block where Will is kept is "often radiant with filtered sun and stippled blue skies. The dirt functioned like a scrim and subtly patterned the light that came through." While Will's conduct in prison is hardly model (he is both brutally manipulative and seductive), the depth of his empathy for his son is stunningly real: "A word about Bo and he felt a kind of bizarre misery. It started in his groin, then radiated down toward the space behind each kneecap with a slow red insistence. It stopped there, rested in an oscillating on-off pattern, then traveled upward again, reaming his hip joints, landing in the center of his sternum. His throat would swell, then his head would finally dry out like a gourd and swing with pain. This choreography was completely reliable."

While there is much else going on in the plot of *Wavemaker II*—particularly the careful evocation of how Roy Cohn became so nefarious, replete with compelling portraits of his mother, his girlfriend, and his own lawyer—the moral force of the novel and its emotional strength evolve from Hughes's treatment of the child's illness and how the world that surrounds him can offer at best only a failing embrace. If the novel is occasionally mechanical and sometimes bloodless, it is also honest. As Will's moral descent deepens, he sees quite clearly and "not for the first time, that the people who waited for him would be better off if he never came home."

Fred Leebron is author of the novels Out West, Six Figures, *and the forthcoming* In the Middle of All This. *He teaches at Gettysburg College and directs the low-residency M.F.A. program at Queens College in Charlotte.*

WATERBORNE *Poems by Linda Gregerson. Houghton Mifflin, $23.00 cloth. Reviewed by H. L. Hix.*

"Eyes Like Leeks," the first poem in Linda Gregerson's new collection, *Waterborne,* distills in a parenthesis the problematic that pervades the poems: "(how / odd / to be this and no other and, like all / / the others, marked for death)." Accident divides us from others and from the parallel lives we might have lived had this or that been different; necessity joins us to death.

Accident sometimes occurs as something nature does to us. For example, genetic accident deprives "My young friend / / —he's seven—" (and apparently autistic) of emotional understanding others acquire effortlessly: he "touched his mother's face last night / and said *It's / wet* and, making the connection he has had / / to learn by rote, *You're sad.* / It's never / not like this for him." Or for his mother. When a later poem refers to the same child, it makes explicit nature's threat: any particular accident is an exception, but accident is the rule. "For want of an ion the synapse was lost. / / For want of a synapse the circuit was lost. / For want / of a circuit, the kingdom, the child, the social / / smile. And this is just one of the infinite means by which / the world / may turn aside." The particular accident that injures you may spare me, but accident will injure us both.

Sometimes, as Gregerson's poems show, accident occurs as what we do to each other. In one poem, the speaker, a doctor in London, recalls his internship in a Boston emergency room, and the night no one came in because the NBA finals had gone to a seventh game and that game into overtime, "and nothing, not a nearly / severed thumb nor classic gallstone, had / been able / to peel these people away till the broadcast / / was over," people who included a "man with his ten-year-old son, the son / cyanotic /

from asthma." Or again, in another poem, referring to an abused child: "You know // what the surgeon found in his scalp? / Pencil lead. / Six broken points of it, puncture wounds // some of them twelve months old."

Whatever the source of accident, necessity always follows, bringing death, a fact that does not deprive us of joy, but does mean we must take joy from a world that doesn't give it freely. "My / hour with you (one / breath, one more) was theft."

That Gregerson so fixedly casts a cold eye on life, on death, puts her out of step with our age. Her awareness that, as Kierkegaard says, "the negative is present in existence" manifests itself in thematic and formal continuities that give *Waterborne* a momentum like the river—one of its recurring metaphors—that gets stronger as it progresses; yet it doesn't overshadow the individual poems, some of which ("Maculate," "Waterborne," "Pass Over," "Cranes on the Seashore," and "Grammatical Mood") will be read and treasured as long as the English language survives. *Waterborne* seeks no consolation, and offers none. Gregerson confronts life as it is, not as she wishes it were. Only on those terms can a poet give her readers, as Gregerson does, the world.

H. L. Hix's most recent poetry collections are Surely as Birds Fly *and* Rational Numbers. *His collection of essays on poetry,* As Easy as Lying, *is forthcoming from Etruscan Press.*

THE CAPRICES *Short stories by Sabina Murray. Mariner Books, $13.00 paper. Reviewed by Debra Spark.*

The Caprices, Sabina Murray's ambitious debut collection of stories, largely concerns the lives of men and women in the Far East in the early forties, which is to say, those who were affected by World War II, either by being orphaned and abandoned (in the case of the characters of the title story, who live in a Japanese-occupied town in the Philippines) or by being direct participants in the war. One story tells of an Anglo-Indian man starving to death in a Singapore prison camp; another of an Italian man from Australia and an Irishman from Boston who are marooned in the jungle with a baseball-loving Japanese prisoner of war. Still another story focuses on the life of an Australian man who survives the war, but never gets beyond the trauma of his time laying railroad track as part of a Thai labor camp. Even when the stories are set in more recent decades, the deprivations of war are never far behind. An American widower living in Massachusetts reencounters the Filipino family who rescued him from a pile of dead men. A Japanese collaborator, living an anonymous life in Manila, becomes embroiled anew with his former accomplice, a man who helped him bury maps that presumably lead to war treasure.

The stories of *The Caprices* are first and foremost about the ironies, humiliations, and brutalities of war. Murray is unsparing in her vision of starvation, death, decapitation, and disease. Heads roll (literally, and often) in this book. Men starve to death, fingers are chopped off of bodies, testicles swell up into large grapefruit because of wet beriberi, and men are shot. Such horror can't be—and isn't—lightened by humor. "Laughter," admits one of the characters, "was strange music." And yet, Murray's tight writing, her powerful sense of story, and her passionate urgency prevent tragedy from subsuming art, from making the book too lugubrious to press on. What tugs one forward—through even the most painful of scenes—is curiosity about where things will end up. Not where things will end up emotionally, exactly, because one knows that in advance, but where things will end up in terms of the stories' unpredictable plots. What *will* happen when the Dutch weapons trader, a longtime expat in Sumatra, reencounters his enemy? What *will* the fate of the war treasure be? Because almost all of Murray's stories are intricately structured between past and present action, one always sees where war leads, where war takes people, as in the remarkable "Order of Precedence," in which a Brit and Anglo-Indian man—once part of the same snobby polo-playing circle—meet again at a POW camp. In the title story, a mad girl engineers a second meeting between herself and her father's murderer. In "Folly," one sees what happens twenty years after an encounter between a warrior, a weapons trader, and his awkward daughter. Perhaps the highest compliment one can pay this collection is that it manages to be intriguing, though emotionally exhausting. It leaves the reader exactly where a war book should: agreeing with the last story's conclusion, "We must all put down our weapons. It is time to stop."

Debra Spark's most recent novel is The Ghost of Bridgetown *(Graywolf, 2001).*

Russell Banks recommends *Senseless,* a novel by Stona Fitch: "A scary, smart moral fable for the post-9/11 U.S. reality, it's short and not at all sweet." (Soho)

George Garrett recommends *Forever Remembered,* interviews edited by Irv Broughton: "This is a wonderful gathering of interviews with World War II combat pilots. Broughton, a poet and filmmaker, is every bit as good as Studs Terkel in eliciting the stories and memories of these old guys." (Eastern Washington)

DeWitt Henry recommends *Deep River: A Memoir of a Missouri Farm,* by David Hamilton: "In an experimental 'memoir' that extends from the personal to the regional to the historic and geographical with an epic sweep comparable to Thoreau's in *Walden* and William Carlos Williams's in *Paterson, New Jersey,* Hamilton considers the legacies of injustice in Missouri as a slave state; in the reconstruction legends of 'bushwhackers'; and in Native American history. Time, space, and the Missouri River are presences that would seem to erase any human history; however, Hamilton's parents and brother emerge as fully imagined, as does the author himself, remarkable for his reverence for language, for story, for the land, and for the legacies of love." (Missouri)

Fanny Howe recommends *Veil,* poems by Rae Armantrout: "A selection of Armantrout's poems from the past twenty years that were published by small presses. Irony, paranoia, passion, written with precision and glitter. A jewel." (Wesleyan)

Philip Levine recommends *Overtime,* poems by Joseph Millar: "If you want the real news of how America lives, of what it's like to be here with us, Joseph Millar is your poet. What are the folks like at Ed's Auto Repair 'that dim cool mine / smelling of gas and iron' or what's it like to be at Hefka's Bar with Thomas Wyatt or at the track at Bay Meadows with Herrick? What's it like outside Monterey when 'night drifts into the artichoke fields / And the swallows veer off toward the hills'? *Overtime* will tell you with exactitude and delicacy in poems like none you've read before. Millar knows a country, an America, that's been here all along waiting for its voice: it's time we listened." (Eastern Washington)

Ellen Bryant Voigt recommends *Changeable Thunder,* poems by David Baker: "David Baker's sixth book combines a flexible syllabic line, a highly idiomatic voice, and a wide range of reference in meditative poems of great intelligence and feeling." (Arkansas)

Ann Beattie, *The Doctor's House,* a novel: A fascinating, emotionally complex chronicle of a Cambridge copyeditor who is mourning her husband's accidental death; her brother, who is seeking out women from high school for sex; and their alcoholic mother—all of them trying to unfetter themselves from the tyrannical doctor who was father and husband. (Scribner)

Robert Boswell, *Century's Son,* a novel: A Midwestern college professor and her activist-turned-garbage-collector husband are riven and bound by their son's suicide ten years before, as well as by their daughter, who's become a teenage mother. Into this exhilarating and penetrating portrait comes the professor's Russian father, who claims to be a century old. (Knopf)

Mark Doty, *Source,* poems: Doty's sixth book of poetry magnificently explores desire and the paradox of selfhood in matters of public life and private struggle, with boldly colored, lyrical scenes from New York, Provincetown, Vermont, and Latin America. (HarperCollins)

Richard Ford, *A Multitude of Sins,* stories: Nine incisive stories and a bravura novella that explicate the sins of adultery and lust. These dramas unfold in Maine, Connecticut, New Orleans, Michigan, and elsewhere with flawless execution. (Knopf)

Donald Hall, *The Painted Bed,* poems: Hall's masterful thirteenth collection of poems expand on the themes of love, death, and mourning. The works here are by turns furious and resigned, spirited and despairing—"mania is melancholy reversed," he writes. (Houghton Mifflin)

Philip Levine, *The Bread of Time: Toward an Autobiography,* personal essays: With artful, witty, illuminating prose, Levine recounts his youth in Detroit and his adulthood in California and Spain, and celebrates his mentors John Berryman and Yvor Winters. (Michigan)

Howard Norman, *The Haunting of L.,* a novel: The final book in Norman's Canadian trilogy, this beautifully crafted novel—set in Manitoba and Halifax—becomes a chilling fable about moral blindness, spirit photography, adultery, artistic ambition, and greed. (FSG)

Maura Stanton, *Do Not Forsake Me, Oh My Darling,* stories: Ten darkly funny short stories that prove to be unpredictable, smart, and lively, with tales ranging from a glimpse of Gertrude Stein playing Ping-Pong with a G.I. in Paris during World War II to a woman discovering that her dead sister had written a bad novel. (Notre Dame)

Ellen Bryant Voigt, *Shadow of Heaven,* poems: Philip Levine submits: "Once again in her poetry, Voigt plumbs the stubbornness of the human spirit and the mysteries of the world in which it lives and dies. Although she surrenders none of her gift for storytelling, this new work is her most lyrical, and as always her lucidity and grace honor the language. This book is her finest: the poems are driven forward by lyrical restraint and by a ferocity of attention that for me is religious." (Norton)

CONTRIBUTORS' NOTES

Spring 2002

ELIZABETH ALEXANDER is the author, most recently, of *Antebellum Dream Book*. She teaches at Yale University.

STEVE ALMOND's debut collection, *My Life in Heavy Metal*, was published in April 2002 by Grove Press. His stories have appeared in *Playboy, Zoetrope, Book, The Missouri Review,* and other magazines. He teaches creative writing at Boston College.

JANE AVRICH's short stories have appeared in *Harper's, The Paris Review, Story,* and *Tin House,* and her collection is forthcoming from Houghton Mifflin. She teaches English at Saint Ann's School in Brooklyn and lives in New York City.

LINDA BAMBER teaches in the English department of Tufts University. She is the author of *Comic Women, Tragic Men: Gender and Genre in Shakespeare.* Her stories, poems, and essays have appeared in *Raritan, The Kenyon Review, Harvard Review, Tikkun, The Nation, The Michigan Quarterly,* and elsewhere.

GEOFFREY BECKER is the author of *Dangerous Men,* a collection of stories, and *Bluestown,* a novel. He is a past winner of the Drue Heinz Literature Prize, the Nelson Algren Award, and an NEA fellowship. His story "Black Elvis" appeared in *The Best American Short Stories 2000.* He teaches at Towson University.

MILAHAIL BORICH has an M.F.A. in writing from the University of California, Irvine. His work has appeared in *The New Yorker, The North American Review, The Paris Review,* and *New Letters,* and his book, *The Black Hawk Songs,* was published in the University of Illinois poetry series.

ANDREA CARTER BROWN's first collection, *Brook & Rainbow,* won the Sow's Ear Press Chapbook Competition and was published in 2001. Her poems are forthcoming this spring in *The Mississippi Review, Many Mountains Moving,* and *The North American Review,* and previously appeared in *The Gettysburg Review* and *The Marlboro Review.*

JULIE BRUCK is the author of two books of poetry, both from Brick Books: *The End of Travel* (1999) and *The Woman Downstairs* (1993). Her poems have appeared in such magazines as *Ms.* and *The New Yorker.* A former Montrealer, she now lives in San Francisco.

JAN CLAUSEN's latest book is a memoir, *Apples and Oranges* (Houghton Mifflin, 1999). She teaches in the Eugene Lang College and Goddard M.F.A. writing programs. "From a Glass House" is the title poem of a new manuscript that includes work published in *Hanging Loose, The Kenyon Review, Luna, Rhino,* and elsewhere.

TOI DERRICOTTE's two most recent books are *Tender,* a volume of poems from the University of Pittsburgh Press that won the 1998 Paterson Poetry Prize, and *The Black Notebooks,* a literary memoir from W.W. Norton that was a *New York Times* Notable Book.

R. ERICA DOYLE is a writer of Trinidadian descent. Her work has appeared in *The Best American Poetry 2001, Role Call, Bum Rush the Page, Callaloo, Ms., Black Issues Book Review,* and *Blithe House Quarterly.* A Cave Canem fellow, she has received awards from the Astraea and Hurston/Wright Foundations.

EUGENE DUBNOV was born in 1949 in Tallinn and educated at the University of Moscow, Bar-Ilan University, Israel, and London University. He has published three volumes of poems in Russian, and his verse and prose have appeared in English in periodicals in Britain, the U.S., and Canada, as well as in French, Hebrew, and German translations.

DENISE DUHAMEL's most recent poetry collection is *Queen for a Day: Selected and New Poems* (Pittsburgh, 2001). The recipient of a 2001 NEA fellowship in poetry, she is an assistant professor at Florida International University in Miami.

JANE EHRLICH is a prize-winning artist who has shown extensively in the Boston area for over twenty years. Her work is in many private and corporate collections. She lives and paints in Cambridge.

MARTÍN ESPADA's sixth book of poems is called *A Mayan Astronomer in Hell's Kitchen* (Norton). His previous collection, *Imagine the Angels of Bread* (Norton), won an American Book Award and was a finalist for the National Book Critics Circle Award. He teaches in the English department at the University of Massachusetts–Amherst.

JULIE FAY's most recent poetry collection is *The Woman Behind You* (Pittsburgh, 1999). She lives in Blounts Creek, North Carolina, and Montpeyroux, France. In the fall of 2002, she will be Resident Director of the study abroad program in Montpellier, France, for East Carolina University and the Kentucky Institute of International Studies.

MARILYN HACKER is the author of nine books of poems, most recently *Squares and Courtyards,* published by W.W. Norton in 2000. *Desesperanto* will appear in the spring of 2003. She is also the translator of several contemporary French poets, including Claire Malroux, Vénus Khoury-Ghata, and Hédi Kaddour. She lives in New York and Paris.

KIMIKO HAHN is the author of seven collections of poetry: *The Artist's Daughter* (forthcoming from W.W. Norton), *Mosquito and Ant, Volatile, The Unbearable Heart* (which was awarded an American Book Award), *Earshot, Air Pocket,* and *We Stand Our Ground* (with Gale Jackson and Susan Sherman).

FORREST HAMER is the author of *Call & Response* (Alice James, 1995), which won the Beatrice Hawley Award, and *Middle Ear* (Roundhouse, 2000), which won the Bay Area Book Reviewers Association Award.

YONA HARVEY is a graduate of Howard University and The Ohio State University. The recipient of a Barbara Deming Award in poetry, she lives in Pittsburgh with her husband and daughter.

LOLA HASKINS's most recent collection of poetry is *The Rim Benders* (Anhinga, 2001). Her work has appeared in *The Atlantic Monthly, The Christian Science Monitor, The London Review of Books, The Beloit Poetry Journal, The Georgia Review, The Southern Review, Prairie Schooner,* and elsewhere.

TERRANCE HAYES's second book of poems, *Hip Logic* (Viking Penguin, 2002), was a National Poetry Series selection in 2001. His debut collection, *Muscular Music* (Tia Chucha, 1999), won the Kate Tufts Discovery Award and a Whiting Writer's Award. He lives in Pittsburgh and teaches creative writing at Carnegie Mellon University.

HONORÉE FANONNE JEFFERS's first book, *The Gospel of Barbecue* (Kent State, 2000), was chosen by Lucille Clifton for the 1999 Stan and Tom Wick Prize for Poetry; her second book of poetry, *Outlandish Blues,* will be published by Wesleyan University Press in 2003. Her poems are forthcoming in *The Kenyon Review, Black Warrior Review,* and *Prairie Schooner.*

TYEHIMBA JESS has been published in *Soul Fires: Young Black Men on Love and Violence* and *Bum Rush the Page.* A former Cave Canem member, he won an Illinois Arts Council Artist Fellowship in Poetry for 2000–01 and the 2001 *Chicago Sun Times* Poetry Award.

HETTIE JONES's first book of poems, *Drive,* won the Poetry Society of America's 1999 Norma Farber Award. Her second, *All Told,* is forthcoming from Hanging Loose this year. Her memoir, *How I Became Hettie Jones,* is available from Grove. She is currently working with Bob Marley's widow, Rita, on a memoir.

PATRICIA SPEARS JONES is the author of the collection *The Weather That Kills,* which was published by Coffee House Press in 1995, and the play *Mother,* which was produced by Mabou Mines in 1994. Her poems have been anthologized most recently in *The Best American Poetry 2000, Blood and Tears: Poems for Matthew Shepard,* and *Real Things: An Anthology of Popular Culture in America.*

A. VAN JORDAN was born and raised in Akron, Ohio. His book, *Rise,* was published by Tia Chucha Press in 2001. He currently lives in the Washington, D.C., metropolitan area.

HÉDI KADDOUR was born in Tunisia, but has lived in France since childhood. He has published three books of poems with Gallimard: *La Fin des vendanges* (1989), *Jamais une ombre simple* (1994), and *Passage au Luxembourg* (2000). Other poems of his, in Marilyn Hacker's translation, have appeared in *APR, The New Yorker, The Paris Review, Poetry, Poetry International, Prairie Schooner,* and *Verse.*

ERIKA KROUSE is the author of a short story collection, *Come Up and See Me Sometime* (Scribner, 2001). Her work has appeared previously in *Ploughshares*, as well as in *The New Yorker, The Atlantic Monthly, Story,* and *Shenandoah*. She lives in Boulder, Colorado, and is working on a novel.

JULIA B. LEVINE's first collection of poems, *Practicing for Heaven*, was the 1998 winner of the Anhinga Prize for Poetry. She has poems published or forthcoming in *Prairie Schooner, The Nation, The Southern Poetry Review, Lullwater Review, Zone 3*, and *Americas Review*. She lives and works as a clinical psychologist in Davis, California.

WILLIAM HENRY LEWIS is the author of a collection of stories, *In the Arms of Our Elders* (Carolina Wren, 1995), and his work has appeared in numerous publications, including *The Best American Short Stories 1996*. Raised in the U.S., Lewis now lives in New Providence Island, Bahamas, where he teaches creative writing and literature at the College of the Bahamas. He is completing his second collection of stories.

PAUL LISICKY is the author of the novel *Lawnboy* (Turtle Point, 1999) and the collection *Famous Builder*, forthcoming from Graywolf Press in the fall of 2002. A recipient of fellowships from the NEA and the Michener/Copernicus Society, he teaches at Sarah Lawrence College and in the low-residency M.F.A. program at Antioch University, Los Angeles.

TIMOTHY LIU is the author of four books of poems, most recently *Hard Evidence* (Talisman, 2001). He is currently on leave from William Paterson University in order to serve as a Visiting Professor at the University of Michigan.

SHARA MCCALLUM is the author of *The Water Between Us*. Her poems and essays have appeared in *The Antioch Review, Callaloo, Creative Nonfiction, Witness*, and *The New American Poets: A Bread Loaf Anthology*. One of her poems was also chosen for Billy Collins's "Poetry 180" project.

KATHLEEN MCGOOKEY's book of poems, *Whatever Shines* (2001), is available from White Pine Press. Poems are forthcoming in *Epoch* and *Willow Springs*.

MAILE MELOY's stories have appeared in *The New Yorker* and *The Paris Review*. Her first story collection, *Half in Love*, is forthcoming from Scribner in July 2002. She lives in California.

SANDELL MORSE has published stories and essays in *Dutiful Daughters, Surviving Crisis, The Green Mountains Review, Iris, Bridges, New England Review, Ploughshares*, and elsewhere. She lives in York, Maine.

GREGORY PARDLO received an M.F.A. at New York University as a *New York Times* Fellow in poetry. He has been awarded fellowships from Cave Canem and the MacDowell Colony. A senior editor of *Painted Bride Quarterly*, he teaches at Parsons School of Design and John Jay College and lives in Manhattan.

ED PAVLIC teaches at Union College and lives in Schenectady, New York. His book of poems, *Paraph of Bone & Other Kinds of Blue,* won the *APR*/Honickman First Book Prize and was published by Copper Canyon Press in 2001. His book of critical essays, *Crossroads Modernism: Descent and Emergence in African-American Literary Culture,* will be published in May 2002 by the University of Minnesota Press.

DANNYE ROMINE POWELL's second collection of poems, *The Ecstasy of Regret,* will be out from the University of Arkansas Press this fall. She has won fellowships from the NEA and the North Carolina Arts Council, and her poems have recently appeared in *Poetry, The Green Mountains Review,* and *Folio.* She is a news columnist for *The Charlotte Observer.*

MINNIE BRUCE PRATT's most recent book of poetry, *Walking Back Up Depot Street,* was named the year's Best Lesbian/Gay Book by *ForeWord: Magazine of Independent Bookstores and Booksellers.* Her second book, *Crime Against Nature,* was a Lamont Poetry Selection of the Academy of American Poets. She can be reached at www.mbpratt.org.

KEVIN PRUFER's second book of poems, *The Finger Bone,* is just out from Carnegie Mellon. He is also editor of *The New Young American Poets* (Southern Illinois, 2000) and *Pleiades: A Journal of New Writing.* He is the recipient of a 2002 Pushcart Prize for poetry.

SHREELA RAY (1942–1994) came to the U.S. from India in 1960 and attended graduate school at the Iowa Writers' Workshop and SUNY–Buffalo. Her poems appeared in many journals, including *The Nation* and *The Dalhousie Review.* The recipient of several awards, she wrote one book in the U.S., *Night Conversations with None Other* (Dustbooks, 1997).

MICHAEL SYMMONS ROBERTS was born in Lancashire, England, in 1963. His most recent collection of poems, *Burning Babylon* (Cape/Random House), was shortlisted for the T. S. Eliot Prize. His work has been widely published and broadcast in the U.K., and he is a regular collaborator with the composer James MacMillan.

NATASHA SAJÉ's first book of poems was *Red Under the Skin* (Pittsburgh, 1994). New poems, essays, and reviews appear in *The Gettysburg Review, The Kenyon Review, The New Republic, Parnassus, Shenandoah,* and *The Writer's Chronicle,* among others. She teaches at Westminster College in Salt Lake City and in Vermont College's M.F.A. in Writing program.

REGINALD SHEPHERD's fourth book, *Otherhood,* is forthcoming from the University of Pittsburgh Press, which also published his other books: *Some Are Drowning* (1993 AWP Award), *Angel, Interrupted,* and *Wrong.* He has received grants and awards from the NEA, the Illinois Arts Council, *The Nation,* and other organizations.

HAL SIROWITZ is the author of two books of poetry, *Mother Said* and *My Therapist Said*, both from Crown. *Mother Said* has been translated into nine languages and was the recipient of a National Jewish Foundation Susan Rose Grant. He is Poet Laureate of Queens, New York.

SANDY SOLOMON's work has appeared in *The New Yorker, The New Republic, The Threepenny Review, The Partisan Review, The Times Literary Supplement,* and elsewhere. Her book, *Pears, Lake, Sun,* winner of the Agnes Lynch Starrett Award, is available in a new edition from the University of Pittsburgh Press.

BRIAN SWANN teaches at Cooper Union in New York City. He has published a number of books, the most recent of which is forthcoming from the University of Nebraska Press: *Voices from Four Directions: Contemporary Translations of the Native Literatures of North America.*

REETIKA VAZIRANI is the author of *World Hotel* (Copper Canyon, 2002) and *White Elephants* (Beacon, 1996). She attended Wellesley College and the University of Virginia. She has received a *Poets & Writers* Exchange Program Award and a Pushcart Prize. Her essay "The Art of Breathing" appears in the anthology *How We Live Our Yoga* (Beacon, 2001). She lives in Trenton, New Jersey.

CHARLES HARPER WEBB's latest book of poems, *Tulip Farms and Leper Colonies,* was published in 2001 by BOA Editions. Among his many awards are the Morse Prize, the Tufts Discovery Award, the Pollak Prize, a Whiting Writer's Award, and a Guggenheim fellowship. He teaches creative writing at California State University, Long Beach.

YOLANDA WISHER is a poet, singer, and cellist living in Philadelphia, where she teaches English at Germantown Friends School. Her poetry has appeared in *The Sonia Sanchez Literary Review, Drumvoices Revue 2000, Meridians, Nocturnes, Fence, Open Letter, Cave Canem VI: 2001 Anthology,* and *POeP!,* one of the first eBook literary journals dedicated to innovative poetry.

SCOTT WITHIAM's poems are forthcoming in *Inkwell, Marlboro Review, Alligator Juniper, Field, Puerto Del Sol, Tar River Poetry,* and *The Laurel Review.*

AL YOUNG is a novelist, poet, essayist, screenwriter, and editor. He is the author of almost twenty books, including the novels *Seduction by Light* and *Who Is Angelina?;* the poetry collections *Heaven* and *The Sound of Dreams Remembered: Poems 1990–2000;* and the musical memoirs *Mingus/Mingus* (with Janet Coleman) and *Drowning in the Sea of Love.*

GUEST EDITOR POLICY *Ploughshares* is published three times a year: mixed issues of poetry and fiction in the Spring and Winter and a fiction issue in the Fall, with each guest-edited by a different writer of prominence, usually one whose early work was published in the journal. Guest editors are invited to solicit up to half of their issues, with the other half selected from unsolicited manuscripts screened for them by staff editors. This guest editor policy is designed to introduce readers to different literary circles and tastes, and to offer a fuller representation of the range and diversity of contemporary letters than would be possible with a single editorship. Yet, at the same time, we expect every issue to reflect our overall standards of literary excellence. We liken *Ploughshares* to a theater company: each issue might have a different guest editor and different writers—just as a play will have a different director, playwright, and cast—but subscribers can count on a governing aesthetic, a consistency in literary values and quality, that is uniquely our own.

～

SUBMISSION POLICIES We welcome unsolicited manuscripts from August 1 to March 31 (postmark dates). All submissions sent from April to July are returned unread. In the past, guest editors often announced specific themes for issues, but we have revised our editorial policies and no longer restrict submissions to thematic topics. Submit your work at any time during our reading period; if a manuscript is not timely for one issue, it will be considered for another. We do not recommend trying to target specific guest editors. Our backlog is unpredictable, and staff editors ultimately have the responsibility of determining for which editor a work is most appropriate. Mail one prose piece or one to three poems. No e-mail submissions. Poems should be individually typed either single- or double-spaced on one side of the page. Prose should be typed double-spaced on one side and be no longer than thirty pages. Although we look primarily for short stories, we occasionally publish personal essays/memoirs. Novel excerpts are acceptable if self-contained. Unsolicited book reviews and criticism are not considered. Please do not send multiple submissions of the same genre, and do not send another manuscript until you hear about the first. *No more than a total of two submissions per reading period.* Additional submissions will be returned unread. Mail your manuscript in a page-size manila envelope, your full name and address written on the outside. In general, address submissions to the "Fiction Editor," "Poetry Editor," or "Nonfiction Editor," not to the guest or staff editors by name, unless you have a legitimate association with them or have been previously published in the magazine. Unsolicited work sent directly to a guest editor's home or office will be ignored and discarded; guest editors are formally instructed not to read such work. All manuscripts and correspondence regarding submissions should be accompanied by a self-addressed, stamped envelope (S.A.S.E.) for a response; no replies will be given by e-mail or postcard. Expect three to five months for a decision. We now receive well over a thousand manuscripts a month. Do not query us until five months have passed, and if you do, please write to us, including an S.A.S.E. and indicating the postmark date of submission, instead of calling or e-mailing. Simultaneous submissions are amenable as long as they are indicated as such and we are notified immediately upon acceptance elsewhere. We cannot accommodate revisions, changes of return address, or forgotten S.A.S.E.'s after the fact. We do not reprint previously published work. Translations are welcome if permission has been granted. We cannot be responsible for delay, loss, or damage. Payment is upon publication: $25/printed page, $50 minimum and $250 maximum per author, with two copies of the issue and a one-year subscription.

~

THE NAME *Ploughshares* 1. The sharp edge of a plough that cuts a furrow in the earth. 2 a. A variation of the name of the pub, the Plough and Stars, in Cambridge, Massachusetts, where the journal *Ploughshares* was founded. 2 b. The pub's name was inspired by the Sean O'Casey play about the Easter Rising of the Irish "citizen army." The army's flag contained a plough, representing the things of the earth, hence practicality; and stars, the ideals by which the plough is steered. 3. A shared, collaborative, community effort that has endured for thirty years. 4. A literary journal that has been energized by a desire for harmony, peace, and reform. Once, that spirit motivated civil rights marches, war protests, and student activism. Today, it still inspirits a desire for beating swords into ploughshares, but through the power and the beauty of the written word.

The St. Louis Poetry Center

42nd Annual Best Poem

Poetry Contest

DEADLINE: MAY 15, 2002

Grand Prize: $2,000

And Publication in: MARGIE/ The American Journal of Poetry

Finalist Judge: LOUISE GLÜCK

Second Prize: $250   Third Prize: $100

Photo (c) Sigrid Estrada
"Fine Literary Portraiture"
NYC 212.673.4300

www.stlouispoetrycenter.org

GUIDELINES
1. Submit up to 3 unpublished poems (60 line limit per poem).
2. Include a cover letter with your name, address, phone & title of each poem. Please, NO names on poems.
3. Enclose a **$15 entry fee** payable to The St. Louis Poetry Center. 4. Additional poems may be submitted at $5 each additional poem.
5. All work will be considered for publication in MARGIE.
6. Entries must be **postmarked by May 15, 2002.** 7. Submit entries to: The St. Louis Poetry Center, 567 North & South Rd., #8, St. Louis, MO 63130. Include SASE for contest results.

James A. Michener Center for Writers

Master of Fine Arts in Writing

DIRECTOR
James Magnuson

ADMIT ONE

University of Texas • Austin • Master of Fine Arts in Writing

Join a selective and close-knit community of writers at a first-rate university in the cultural mecca that is Austin, Texas. Fellowships of $17,500 granted annually to all students enrolled in our three-year program.

It's your ticket to write.

UT Michener Center for Writers
702 E. Dean Keeton St. • Austin, TX 78705

512/471.1601 • www.utexas.edu/academic/mcw

RESIDENT & RECENT VISITING FACULTY

Playwriting	*Screenwriting*	*Poetry*	*Fiction*
Ruth Margraff	Robert Foshko	Judith Kroll	Michael Adams
Suzan Zeder	Stephen Harrigan	Khaled Mattawa	Laura Furman
Lee Blessing	Charles Ramirez-Berg	David Wevill	Zulfikar Ghose
Sherry Kramer	William Hauptman	Thomas Whitbread	Elizabeth Harris
Spring 2002	Anne Rapp	August Kleinzahler	Rolando Hinojosa-Smith
Naomi Iizuka	*Fall 2001*	Heather McHugh	Peter LaSalle
	Tim McCanlies	*Fall 2001*	J.M. Coetzee
		Naomi Shihab Nye	Anthony Giardina
			James Kelman
			Fall 2001
			Joy Williams
			Spring 2002
			Denis Johnson

THE UNIVERSITY OF TEXAS AT AUSTIN

BENNINGTON WRITING SEMINARS

MFA in Writing and Literature
Two-Year Low-Residency Program

A. BLAKE GARDNER

FICTION
NONFICTION
POETRY

Jane Kenyon Poetry Scholarships available
For more information contact:
Writing Seminars
Box PL
Bennington College
Bennington, VT 05201
802-440-4452, Fax 802-440-4453
www.bennington.edu/bencol/writing/mfa.htm

The Academy of American Poets Announces

NATIONAL POETRY MONTH APRIL 2002

Celebrating the 100th anniversary of the birth of Langston Hughes

Visit www.poets.org and discover
a special Langston Hughes Centenary Exhibit

National Poetry Month is sponsored this year by the following organizations:

CHAIRMAN'S CIRCLE: Alfred A. Knopf, Inc. • Appleton Coated Papers • Bennett Book Advertising, Inc. • Gale Research • Merriam-Webster • The National Endowment for the Arts • The New York Times Advertising Dept. • Random House, Inc. • Scholastic, Inc. • United States Postal Service

BENEFACTORS: ECM Records • Farrar, Straus & Giroux • Harcourt • HarperCollins Publishers • HarperCollins Children's Books • Houghton Mifflin • Ladan Reserve Press • Northwestern University Press

PREMIUM SPONSORS: American Booksellers Association (ABA) • American Library Association (ALA) • Associated Writing Programs • Beacon Press • BOA Editions, Ltd. • Bright Hill Press • City Lights Books • Copper Canyon Press • Council of Literary Magazines & Presses • Curbstone Press • Four Way Books • Geraldine R. Dodge Foundation • Graywolf Press • Grove/Atlantic • Hanging Loose Press • Kelsey Street Press • Library of America • Louisiana State University Press • Miami University Press • Milkweed Editions • Modern Language Association • NACSCORP • NCTE • New Directions • New Issues Press (New Issues Poetry & Prose) • Oberlin College Press/FIELD • Pearl Street Publishing, LLC • Penguin Books • Poetry Society of America • Poets & Writers • Robinson Jeffers Tor House Foundation • Sarabande Books • Scholastic, Inc. • Scribner • Teachers & Writers Collaborative • University of Akron Press • University of Chicago Press • University of Iowa Press • University of Massachusetts Press • University of Pittsburgh Press • University of Wisconsin Press • Urban Libraries Council • W.W. Norton • Wesleyan University Press

MEDIA SPONSORS: AGNI • American Book Review • American Poet • The American Poetry Review • Antioch Review • The Atlantic Monthly • Black Warrior Review • Bloomsbury Review • Bomb • Fence • Five Points • Georgia Review • Harper's • Hudson Review • jubilat • Kenyon Review • Library Journal • The Nation • New England Review • The New Republic • The New York Review of Books • night rally • The North American Review • Northwest Review • Open City • Osiris • Paris Review • Ploughshares • Poetry Flash • Publishers Weekly • Salmagundi • Seneca Review • The Sewanee Review • School Library Journal • Shenandoah • Washington Square Literary Journal • The Writer's Chronicle • ZYZZYVA

Photographs—Photograph of Langston Hughes in fedora by Carl Van Vechten, with the permission of the Van Vechten Trust; photograph of Langston Hughes at typewriter by Marvin and Morgan Smith. All photographs courtesy of Photographs and Prints Division, Schomburg Center for Research in Black Culture. The New York Public Library, Astor, Lenox, and Tilden Foundations. *Manuscripts*—Manuscripts, Archives and Rare Books Division, Schomburg Center for Research in Black Culture, The New York Public Library, Astor, Lenox and Tilden Foundations. Langston Hughes Collection. *Poems*—"To You" and "The Negro Speaks of Rivers" are reprinted with permission of the Langston Hughes Estate.

HARD BREAD

PEG BOYERS

"Boyers has written the poetry of *another person*, an operation requiring the paired gifts of ventriloquist and vampire. The explicit wisdom and the mysterious reticence of 'Natalia Ginzburg' constitutes, for all Peg Boyers' modesty of address, the most original debut in my experience of contemporary American poetry."
—Richard Howard

"Boyers inhabits the soul of Natalia Ginzburg and, in poems of rare power, illuminates the inner lives of Ginzburg's intimates, those who wrote their way through the horrors of fascism, imprisonment and survival...a masterpiece of lyric dramatic art."
—Carolyn Forché

"The creation of the voice in this book—stoic, resigned, insistent on truth—is a brilliant achievement ... Read Peg Boyers' book and you will never forget it."
—Frank Bidart

"This is true poetry, giving voice with unforgettable specificity to the woe, comedy and heroism of a twentieth-century life."
—Robert Pinsky

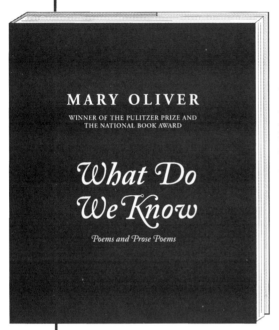